MR GILTROW'S E⸺

A WALK THROUGH WHITTON HISTORY

Ed Harris

Phantom Books

Published by Phantom Books
P O Box 295
Twickenham
TW2 7WU

Copyright 2005 © by Ed Harris

British Library Cataloguing in Publication Data
A catalogue record for this book is available from the British Library.

ISBN 0-9551486-0-X

Printed in Great Britain by Tandem Press
www.tandempress.com

CONTENTS

Introduction 5

Mr Giltrow Prepares 11

Kneller Road from Chase Bridge to Hounslow Road............................17

Hounslow Road from Whitton Park to Holly Bush Corner..................65

Nelson Road (west) to Hanworth Road..101

Hanworth Road to The Gunpowder Mills...121

Powder Mill Lane to Hospital Bridge Road 137

Hospital Bridge Road to Holly Bush Corner......................................145

Nelson Road (east) to Kneller Road..163

Culmination and conclusions 191

Sources & further Reading 200

Acknowledgements..204

Index 205

INTRODUCTION

'Whitton is Richmond's cheapest area and set to the west of the borough. A mixture of mid-war detached, semis and terraces predominate although a few Victorian cottages can be found in Whitton Dean. House prices are influenced by distance from the busy Chertsey Road'. Thus in three sentences did one local estate agent discount an entire physical landscape, all of its history and material artefacts, and provide the inspiration for this book.

As suburbia is widely recognised as the least studied subject of the past, so Local history is also something of an enigma. Is it a serious academic discipline or an eccentric pastime like train spotting? Or does it provide a useful platform for the smaller worlds we mostly all inhabit within the wider context of what 'real' historians like to call 'Big History'?

1901 was a lean year for Big History. Britain's longest reigning monarch was dead. The Boer War was raging, the Metropolitan Police adopted fingerprinting and the vacuum cleaner was invented. But for the 1,000 or so men, women and children comprising the tiny rural community of Whitton in West Middlesex, it marked the beginning of the end of a way of life largely unchanged for centuries.

The census enumeration is an inventory of the entire population taken every 10 years to include details such as residence, age, sex, occupation, marital status, birth history, and relationship to the head of household. It is a method used for accumulating statistical data such as demographic, social, and economic information pertaining to a population at a specific time. Sunday was originally chosen as Census Night, as it was traditionally the day of least population movement. John Burridge Giltrow was the census enumerator for Whitton in 1901. Walking in his footsteps, meeting the people he met and the places he saw provides a unique peg upon which to hang an entire history, past and present, big and small of this otherwise unremarkable place.

Mr Giltrow described his route across the 888-acre ward as: '...commencing at Chase Bridge to the post office, The Married Quarters & Lodge (not including Kneller Hall), a cottage at the Riding School, Whitton Park, then from the Vicarage to the Nelson Inn including Heathfield Farm & two cottages near the Railway Cottage near Hounslow Station. Mr & Mrs Clarke's House, The Lodge at Hounslow Cemetery, two cottages in the Hounslow Road, all the houses & Lodge at the Gunpowder Mills, The Lodge at Twickenham Cemetery, The Cottage occupied by Mr Lever, Percy Road, Nelson Road to Mr Mann's Inclusive.'

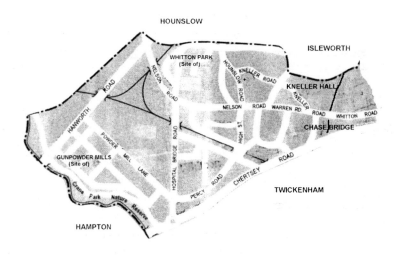

The route today remains unchanged to include the whole of Kneller Road from Chase Bridge towards Hounslow Road and the site of Whitton Park; south along Hounslow Road, past the church of St Philip & St James, to Holly Bush Corner and then west on Nelson Road as far as Hanworth Road and from there as far south as Crane Park. East along Powder Mill Lane to Percy Road as far as The Admiral Nelson and then Nelson Road (east) from Holly Bush Corner towards Whitton Village and Kneller Road.

When Queen Victoria died, Mr Giltrow in common with most Britons and half a pink-tinted globe had never lived under another monarch. While the vast majority of his fellow countrymen continued to live miserable, grinding lives, John Burridge Giltrow had inched above that station. His expression of civic duty in becoming a Census Enumerator shows enterprise and endeavour, although the quality and types of individual attracted to the role was no indicator of his proficiency.

The Times reported in 1861 that applications for the post of Census Enumerator 'were exceedingly numerous and instances occur in which clergymen, scripture readers and others, influenced by philanthropic motives, have expressed a desire to enumerate districts inhabited by the poorer classes'. In 1891, the Superintendent of Statistics at the General Register Office felt that the enumerators were 'on the whole rather a poor lot...very unsatisfactory...their mere handwriting and the general aspect of their work showed that a great many of them were very illiterate men.'

In seeking John Giltrow, we find four males sharing the same name recorded in the 1901 census. One was a 24-year-old Master Baker and his 10-year-old son, also called John, living in Dunstable. The third was a 53-year-old quarry worker living in Bristol, and the fourth was a 26-year-old insurance agent, born in Buckinghamshire, married to Alice two years his senior at age 28 and living a mile from Whitton at 190 High Street, Hounslow. With the all-important initial 'B' for Burridge included in his name, the said John B Giltrow is hereby declared enumerator for the entire parish of Whitton, 1901.

In so doing, he was following a tradition begun in 1801 and which, except for 1941 due to the Second World War, had been carried out across the United Kingdom every ten years. The first four censuses were little more than simple head counts of the population collected on a parish basis with no details on households. Forms were distributed to each parish where the overseers of the poor, substantial landholders and the local clergy were responsible for providing information on the number of people in the parish, their employment, the number of inhabited and uninhabited houses in the parish and how many families occupied them.

Once collected the data was sent to the Home Office for the results to be collated prior to being laid before Parliament. Age was included in 1821 to assess numbers of men able to bear arms, and to improve the tables upon which life assurance was based. More detailed questions on occupations from 1831 provided the government with economic information, but the first meaningful exercise was held in 1841 wherein the head of each household was required to complete a census schedule, or form, that gave the name, age, sex, occupation and place of birth of each individual at home on Census Night.

In 1851, questions were added about the relationship of each individual to the head of the household. Included for the first time were those living on vessels in inland waterways or at sea and those in the armed forces overseas or British subjects residing or working abroad. Later additions included employment status and any disabilities such as lunatic, imbecile or feeble-minded, and in 1891 how many rooms were habitable if less than five.

The whole process began with a census enumerator distributing a form, or schedule, to each household in his District before Census Night. The householder was required to complete the form, declaring who was under their roof on that night, including visitors. From the following Monday, the enumerator returned to collect the completed schedule. If it was not correctly completed, then he was supposed to ask for any information missing. If the householder was unable to fill in the schedule, perhaps because they were illiterate, then the enumerator filled it in for them.

Few of the homes visited by John Burridge Giltrow enjoyed proper sanitation and none had access to electricity. Gas was widely used, although many families still depended on coal-fired ranges or open fires for their cooking. Outside lavatories still produced the 'night soil' used to fertilise the land upon which Whitton's agrarian economy depended. Mass-produced furniture was increasingly available on credit, but most homes were poorly furnished with only the very basics. Anything approaching quality was more often than not deposited at the pawnshop to see the family through another week.

Overcrowding was officially numbers over eight persons per household, but typical of Mr Giltrow's experience would be as many or more inhabiting two dank, unwholesome rooms. Piped water in Whitton was a luxury available to the few. The communal tap or access to a well was still common. Only in the growing towns of Twickenham to the south and Hounslow to the north would there soon be the luxury of public baths and washhouses. The various Housing of the Working Classes Acts sought to improve the moral and physical condition of the lower orders, and in 1901 housing was receiving more attention than ever before, although Mr Giltrow would witness precious little improvement in Whitton.

The Bank Holiday Act of 1871 allowed for the first time, ordinary working people access to free time, and entrepreneurs to their disposable income. Sport and recreational pursuits blossomed towards the end of the nineteenth century and getting dressed up to the nines on a Sunday or a Bank Holiday was an event eagerly awaited by the working poor whose forefathers could only have dreamed of such hedonism.

In 1901 the woman's place was still very much in the home. Domestic chores involved a never-ending round of cooking, washing, scrubbing and ironing. If not out working in the fields, washday was a full day's work, often involving taking the children out of school. Many a widow took in washing and ironing to make ends meet. As domestic servants, girls and younger women were employed in the larger households comprising the new middle classes occupying the villas seeding the suburbs.

John Burridge Giltrow would be the last Enumerator to record a section of the population on the cusp of the many social and economic changes evolving elsewhere. A century on and walking in his footsteps we are able to appreciate the scrap of humanity that was Old Whitton and create from it a sense of place. Not just as it appeared on the night of 31st March 1901, but how it came to be, for what reasons, and how the changes over centuries have failed to purge the village from the suburb.

MR GILTROW PREPARES

On the front page of his Censor Enumeration Book, or CEB, John Burridge Giltrow describes his patch as being 'on the north by the Boundary of Isleworth Parish, on the East by the Boundary of Isleworth Parish, on the South by the River Colne and on the west by the Hanworth Road'. Sadly, the naming of any river in this locality is to immediately fall foul of borrowed historical 'fact'. The River Colne that Mr Giltrow refers to is in fact The River Crane, another waterway altogether that winds its way from its source near either Northolt or Hayes or between Pinner and Harrow, depending on the view of whichever past antiquarian you choose. Beyond dispute is that The Crane discharges into the Thames at Isleworth and in so doing, forms the underbelly of Whitton's border.

The other ancient watercourse creating Whitton's northern boundary is Birket's Brook, a once substantial river that continues to trickle underground from its source in Heston to emerge above ground and join the River Crane in St Margarets. Before then its passage is rudely interrupted by the Duke of Northumberland's River, an artificial waterway cut from the Colne in the 16th century to power the water mills at Isleworth Syon. The section running north beside Twickenham Rugby Ground has formed Whitton's eastern boundary since that time. Chase Bridge crossing The Duke's River at this point bisects Whitton Road in Twickenham parish and Kneller Road in Whitton.

The bridge, a narrow, humped-back affair in 1901, probably takes its name from William Chase, a one time sergeant at arms to King Henry VIII, who owned 218 acres of land in the area, including four acres called Chase Close, a substantial property portfolio of 12 cottages and a 'capital' house. At the time of Mr Giltrow's enumeration, The Hon. Charles Seale Hayne, M.P, Liberal Member of Parliament for Ashburton under Gladstone, owned a third of all Whitton Land or that partly contained in the boroughs of Twickenham and Isleworth.

11

Until the 1890s Whitton's manorial rights were divided with the Earl Percy at Syon Park as chief landowner with control of The Duke of Northumberland's River and all of its crossings, including Chase Bridge, for centuries the most direct route linking Twickenham and Hounslow. Between these emerging towns sat the tiny village of Whitton. In 1901 Chase Bridge was proving just as unsuitable for omnibus traffic as it would be inadequate in taking one of the new 'electric car routes' proposed for the fast expanding towns of West Middlesex. The London General Omnibus Company did consider experimenting with a new type of single-decker bus that could manage the bridge and Whitton's tortuous road system. But with the paucity of potential passengers along the route it was felt that the service wouldn't pay and so was dropped. By whatever means Mr Giltrow made his way to each of the 210 households thinly spread throughout Whitton's 888 acres, public transport was not an option.

The Chase Bridge, Kneller Hall.

Today a census enumerator can expect to visit around 450 house-holds. They are given a map of their patch together with a list of all the properties recorded in the last Census, which are updated for any known changes. Their first task is to walk the route and check whether the dwellings still exist and note any new houses that have been added for the occupants to be included in the Census.

In 1901, the Census form was a single sheet of paper, not the bulky document issued today. Unlike the bright yellow pantechnicon bearing the Census Logo the modern enumerator is required to carry, John Burridge Giltrow would have managed his entire quota of forms in a satchel or brief case. He was also unlikely to have been weighed down with today's equivalent of a small stationary store's-worth of expenses claim forms, time sheets, envelopes, explanation leaflets, advice notes and a book to remind enumerators how to deliver the forms and the proper 'doorstep routine'.

If there was no reply at a house, Mr Giltrow would have left a note saying that he had called and would return later. But given the nature of most peoples' work, mostly out from dawn until dusk, this would have resulted in numerous repeat visits or, in the absence of a Team Leader in those days ensuring quality control, he might have recorded 'not at home' against the names of persistent stragglers. Due credit must be afforded John Burridge Giltrow, however, in that his sense of duty was manifest in his fulsome results.

Like his modern day counterparts, Mr Giltrow's first task in the enumeration process was to prepare the forms for delivery, complete with reference and area numbers. Today the name and address of the occupant is supposed to be taken on the doorstep at the point of delivery, but some enumerators decide to do this before setting out to save time. The most important element is to personally hand over the form and ask the householder to ensure it is filled in on Census Night.

Collection of the forms follows as far as possible the same route as previously taken to ensure that all the forms are returned. Mr Giltrow had less than half the numbers of homes to visit than some of his modern equivalents, but even so his patch would have taken at least three or four hours to follow, allowing for checking the information and possibly having to fill in the form himself because of illiteracy.

Living about a mile away in Hounslow, Mr Giltrow was familiar with the ways of rural life, the hours worked in the fields by whom, doing what work at which time of the year. This was important, as the vast majority of the households in Whitton were those of market garden and agricultural workers. It was early spring and they were busy. Also there were few shops and businesses in the village where the head of the household was likely to be found at home during the day.

Many of the women folk would be up and about before the break of dawn, lighting fires and preparing what there was for breakfast. Often they would be joining the men at work in the fields or sheds by 8am. Some rushed home around midday to prepare another meal and again once darkness fell. There was only one optimum time for finding most heads of household at home and that was Sunday.

With the least impact on his own livelihood, Mr Giltrow would have set out first to deliver his schedules on Sunday 25th March 1901. Stragglers or those not at home on that day could be followed up the following Sunday prior to Census Night itself. Collection would have taken place between Sunday 8th and Sunday 15th April, the day that Mr Giltrow signed off his enumeration.

From his home in High Street, Hounslow, the route towards Chase Bridge and the start of the enumeration was straight forward enough. Given the mobility of his occupation as an Insurance Agent, Mr Giltrow was in all probably familiar with Whitton and no doubt some of its inhabitants. Even so, he would have been hard-pressed to call on everyone across such a convoluted route within a reasonable length of time on foot.

It's doubtful he owned one of the three and a quarter million horses at work in Britain in 1901, or enjoyed the sort of income to hire one of over a million commercial carriages and traps. Then the horse still carried more goods than the railways. Fifty years on and there would still be more horses than tractors used on British farms.

The motorcar was still very much a luxury item in 1901 affordable by only the very wealthy and even then used generally for pleasure rather than business, although increasingly popular with doctors. At the turn of the last century there were less than 20,000 cars on Britain's roads and their regulation was hotly contested. Until the petrol-powered internal combustion engine gained dominance in 1910, steam was still the most viable candidate for powering automobiles, introduced ten years earlier when the French enjoyed the major share of the British market.

The 1890s also saw a phenomenal growth in the popularity of cycling, after Scotsman John Boyd Dunlop introduced the pneumatic tyre. The rear freewheel followed shortly afterwards, which enabled the rider to coast without the pedals spinning out of control. This in turn led to the invention of Derailleur gears and cable-pull brakes. By 1895, 50,000 people were employed in bicycle manufacture, although it wouldn't be until around 1905 that the likes of John Burridge Giltrow had access to the first affordable means of personal transport in history.

Protecting his high-buttoned suit against the worst excesses of the weather, Mr Giltrow might have been thankful to one Thomas Burberry, as the weeks prior to Census Night were bitterly cold, beginning with a slight fog, which changed to sleet and then to blinding snowstorms that lasted until a heavy frost lined the roads with a treacherous coating of ice. In 1879, Burberry patented a waterproof cloth impervious to rain, which did not go hard in cold weather or sticky in the heat, or give off a noxious odour peculiar to the earlier voluminous and unwieldy garment developed by Charles Mackintosh.

Thomas Burberry opened his first shop in London in 1891, selling all types of clothes for field sports made from his revolutionary material known as Gaberdine. Thus suitably equipped and protected, John Burridge Giltrow left his home at 190, High Street, Hounslow and walked the 100 yards or so west towards Bell Road for the Whitton Road, en route for the start of his enumeration some twenty minutes away.

KNELLER ROAD FROM CHASE BRIDGE TO HOUNSLOW ROAD.

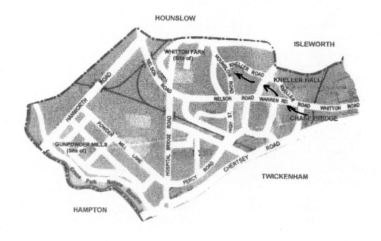

All the houses in that part of the Parish on the east and north of the Isleworth Boundary commencing at Chase Bridge to the post office, The Married Quarters & Lodge (not including Kneller Hall), a cottage at the Riding School....

With one or two exceptions, the names and numbers of houses and road names in Whitton are not given in census returns prior to 1891. The road names in use today didn't come about until after 1878 and had only just entered the popular vernacular by 1901. Whitton Road, once the main highway linking Hounslow and Twickenham, still exists in two parts; that taken by Mr Giltrow from Bell Road in Hounslow as far as the junction with Whitton Dene, and the other section east of Chase Bridge towards Twickenham (pictured below).

This rare photograph taken from the brow of Chase Bridge in 1903 documents a particularly serious episode of flooding by the Duke of Northumberland's River, which covered a vast area of the district from Coles Bridge in Twickenham to St Margarets. Communications with the Duke's Estate about taking steps to prevent flooding in the region had been ongoing since 1892 and was not resolved until 1928. The particularly waterlogged area on the north side of Whitton Road (left) complete with its grove of walnut trees is now the Rugby Football Union's West Car Park. Of the farm buildings opposite, all but one of the mid-nineteenth century cottages behind the stone barn survive from this rural scene.

The aftermath of the same disaster, showing Kneller Road west towards the direction of Whitton. The carts were used either side of the bridge at the height of the flood to convey people along the road from Whitton to Twickenham. To the right is now the site of Chase Bridge Junior School and further west the grounds of Kneller Hall. To the south (left) is now all inter-war housing.

In 1881, the enumerator for Whitton began his audit here with James Walker, a 44-year-old Scot from Lanarkshire who settled in the area sometime before 1880 when Thomas, the youngest of his nine children was born. His wife, Jane, was born in Lanarkshire, as were the couple's other sons and daughters. James Walker employed ten men, three boys and four women on his 39 acre market garden holding, which stretched from Rosecroft Gardens in Twickenham as far west as present day Alton Gardens in Whitton. The farmhouse was scheduled as Garden Cottage in 1891 when it was unoccupied. It failed to appear in 1901 and so called for an immediate deviation on the part of Mr Giltrow at the start of his enumeration.

The Lodge formerly stood at the south entrance gates to The Royal Military School of Music. It appears on a map attaching a sales catalogue dated 1841, but not in any census return prior to 1901, and nor should it have done, for it was the duty of Colonel Barrington-Foote, as Commandant of the said Institution at that time, to make a record separate from that of the civil Census Enumerator.

Not that the Colonel appears to have been a slave to protocol, recently demanding of the local council to have the ditch running alongside the Lodge Gates thoroughly cleaned out. In his reply, the Town Clerk explained that 'scouring, cleansing and keeping open ditches in or through any lands or ground adjoining or lying near to any highway, rests with the owner or occupier; in this instance the War Office'. For reasons best known to himself, John Burridge Giltrow entered into his schedule the names of Charles F Gillam, a 36 -year-old Feltham-born Private in the Royal Fusiliers, his wife Annie and their two children, Edward and Victoria. Crossing over to the south side of Kneller Road, Mr Giltrow re-established physical continuity with previous enumerations and met with the penchant for owners or occupiers to change the names of their dwellings from one census to the next.

Variously recorded as Alton Villa and Grosmont is the large house glimpsed in the distance from Chase Bridge. Just visible above the brow of the bridge is the rooftop of Alton Cottage, now replaced by numbers 47-49 Kneller Road. Manfred Arlotte and his wife Mary moved here from St Marylebone to Whitton in 1894, where the eldest of their three daughters, Beatrice, was born. Their move typified the experience of hundreds of market garden workers forced to flee the Capital to find work elsewhere in the face of rapid housing expansion. Manfred Arlotte probably worked for Decimus Clarke, a prominent local market gardener, who occupied the much grander Alton Villa with his wife Elizabeth. Decimus Clarke was also a leading political figure locally and the first to propose a separate ward for Whitton.

Despite his efforts, Whitton would have to wait until 1910 when the County Council was satisfied that a prima facie case had been made for the alteration of Wards, which resulted in the district divided into five wards for future elections. The Central, East, South and West Wards were each allotted six councillors, with the fifth, Whitton Ward, just the one, commensurate with the scantiness of its population.

By 1901 Decimus Clarke had moved on and Alfred Wilson, Chief Clerk to the Borough Council, appeared as the head of the household, having changed the name from Alton Villa to 'Grosmont' (rooted in the Order of Grandimont begun in King John's reign). Born in Kentish Town in 1859, his wife Sarah a year earlier in Pimlico, the couple arrived in Hounslow in 1892 where their son, also called Alfred, was born. As did the Clarkes before them, the Wilsons maintained a domestic servant. Today, only parts of the villa's original boundary walls survive, enclosing a block of flats called 'Salliesfield'. To the northwest was a two-acre meadow fronting a far more imposing edifice named after the greatest master of the English baroque portrait, Sir Godfrey Kneller.

The building we see today is the last of three large houses to occupy the site and mostly dates from between 1780 and 1850, built of red brick and faced with Bath stone dressing with a plinth around the base of Portland stone. Edmund Cooke built the first house between 1635 and 1646, then the largest mansion in Twickenham, boasting 20 hearths, or fireplaces.

Under the Act of 1662, brought about to reorganise the revenues of the crown following the Restoration, a tax was imposed on the number of fireplaces per household, known as the Hearth Tax. In 1664 there were just 120 houses found liable for Hearth Tax in Whitton compared to 1,015 in Twickenham and 1,381 in Isleworth. The national average was twice as many one-hearth houses as those with two. Twickenham, Isleworth and Heston were all above the national average, but in Whitton there were more one-hearth houses than those with two.

Following a series of owners in the second half of the 17th century, Sir Godfrey Kneller bought the house in 1709 and demolished it to build his own, reputedly with drawings by Sir Christopher Wren. Originally an elegant house in the Queen Anne style, the road passing it was diverted from a gentle curve to follow the meandering course it takes today. Kneller spent the summer months at Whitton, visited and courted by many people of distinction and honour including members of the Royal family. When he died in 1723, the house passed to his widow, Lady Susan, and on her death in 1729, the estate was leased out until 1757 when it was sold to Sir Samuel Prime, a prominent London lawyer, who set about extending the house and engaging in 1795/6 the services of the celebrated garden designer Humphrey Repton to improve the grounds. Much of these works survived until the 1960s when the lake was eventually drained.

The original walls surrounding the property and several houses opposite were demolished to extend its pleasure grounds until by 1818 they reached as far as the present Chertsey Road. The most significant building demolished was that built by Baron John Belasyse of Worlaby in 1687. Only a fraction of the Belasyse's site survives as the grassed wedge at the junction of Kneller and Warren Road, which was cut in the 1930s. The rest is buried under twentieth century semi-detached maisonettes currently ruining the view from Kneller Hall. Remarkably there are no pictures or illustrations of Belasyse's mansion, once the centre of Catholicism in Whitton.

The second son of Thomas, First Lord Fauconburg, Balasyse joined the King at Oxford on the outbreak of the Civil War when he was created Baron. He raised six regiments of horse and foot at his own cost and took part in the major battles of the war. Re-emerging at the Restoration, he was unable as a Catholic to take the Oath of Conformity and was imprisoned in the Tower of London from 1678 until 1684 on the false information that he, with others, was planning to raise a Catholic army. The house eventually came to Belasyse's daughter Mary who was married to another catholic, Robert Constable, 3rd Viscount Dunbar.

A year after his death in 1714, the house was sold to trustees acting for Nathaniel Pigott, a barrister and avowed Catholic, and as such debarred from university or appearance in any court of law. Whitton was then just outside of the 10-mile catholic exclusion zone from the Capital. A couple of miles away was the home of Pigott's great friend, the celebrated satirist and letter writer, Alexander Pope, who had also moved to Twickenham for reasons of his faith.

Ralph, Pigott's son, married the daughter of the 9th Viscount Fairfax of Gilling. Their son, Charles, inherited the estates and assumed the name Fairfax. He was admitted to the Whitton property in 1761, which he retained until about 1778 when it was sold to Samuel Prime who then set about demolishing it, leaving a farmhouse, fore court, agricultural buildings and walled kitchen garden. Morris Emmanuel purchased large parts of the estate in 1846 and on his death in 1894 the property was divided up.

By 1901, the War Department had acquired the walled garden (just visible bottom left in this aerial view) as an enclosure for The Married Quarters attaching The Military School of Music, Kneller Hall.

The four blocks housed the same number of families attached to the school as before, but in clean, modern units of between three and five rooms. While this move freed up accommodation predominantly for agricultural and market garden labourers establishing themselves in the village, their living conditions remained pitiful. The Married Quarters were demolished when the Ministry of Defence built the more modern accommodation comprising Duke of Cambridge Close near Chase Bridge. The blocks of flats nestling inside the original 18th century walled enclosure today are now privately owned. The building attaching the northeast corner of the walled enclosure survives today much as Mr Giltrow would have found it, except for its yellow stock brickwork now painted cream. The Duke of Cambridge public house, built around 1850, was originally a domestic dwelling known as Emma's Cottage.

Stephen Woodland of the Phoenix Brewery, Twickenham, entered into an agreement with Eliza Emmanuel, 'widow, of Paris, France,' to rent the cottage from Lady Day (25 March) 1857 for the yearly rent of 30 pounds to carry on the trade of Beer seller or Licensed Victualler. This was agreed to with the proviso that the trade was 'carried out in such a way and manner as not to cause any noise or disturbance which may be considered or deemed a nuisance or annoyance to such persons as are resident in the immediate neighbourhood.'

William Daniel Norris was trading here in 1859; followed two years later by James Twogood, a beer retailer from Devon when the premises is first named The Duke of Cambridge. Kelly's Directory for 1865 gives Mrs Elizabeth Cherrett as landlady of the Duke of Cambridge Public House, although it was then still a beer house. Charles Notts, Beer Seller, followed on in 1866 with the Rate Book for that year showing Mrs Emmanuel still the owner of the property. Thomas Peck from Clerkenwell is recorded in the census of 1871 as Beerhouse Keeper of The Duke of Cambridge and as Landlord in the 1874 and 1876 editions of Kelly's Directory. Gloucestershire born John Groves was the Beerhouse Keeper in 1881.

The nineteenth century witnessed an unprecedented growth of public drinking houses in England and Wales. The reason for this was the passing of the Beerhouse Act in 1830, which permitted any ratepayer who paid a guinea to the Excise Office to sell home-brewed beer out of their living rooms. The object of the Act was to curb the working classes' excessive consumption of spirits by eradicating gin shops and promoting the 'healthier' alternative of beer, which was thought to be less conducive to drunk and disorderly behaviour.

Within three months of the Act being passed, over 24,000 licences had been issued in England and Wales, but despite the good intentions of the Beerhouse Act these new establishments were condemned for the type of clientele they attracted and for being unhygienic and unruly. To remedy this, the Government introduced a second Act in 1834, which categorised publicans' licences into three types: a full publican's licence, which was granted each year by the local magistrates, and Beerhouses, which were divided into 'on' and 'off' premises sales. Increasingly stricter controls followed as further legislation was introduced regarding licensing, gaming, brewing, and opening hours.

The event of the year for working men in Whitton (pictured over-leaf) as elsewhere in 1900s Britain was 'the Beano', which took place on the last Saturday of August after the men had been paying in for months for the cost of the outing. The local employers and personal friends hired a horse-drawn brake with their men follow-ing on in larger wagons smoking their twopenny cigars and with one or two drinks inside them. Whatever was left after the hire of the brakes and the cost of the dinner would be shared out after the dinner or on return home.

Richard Chance was manning the pumps of the Duke of Cambridge when Mr Giltrow called by. The 45-year-old Beer Retailer had moved into the four-roomed accommodation with his wife, Mary, from Bradford in Yorkshire where their two sons, Edward, aged 18 and George, aged seven were born. Edward was a tarpaulin maker employed in his own right, as were the two boarders, Frank Allen and Francis Hawkin from Staffordshire and Bradford respectively.

When Stephens Woodlands decided to open his Beer House in 1857, he did not do so as purely a speculative venture. Rather he was an astute businessman, for that was the same year the Military School of Music was established at Kneller Hall, holding the promise of 150 student bandsmen on the doorstep looking regularly to quench their thirst. The Government acquired the estate in 1845 as a train-ing college for teachers of pauper and criminal children. Following controversy over its educational methods, the school closed in 1856 when it was acquired by the War Department as a school to teach music to army bandsmen, taking as its guiding force Queen Victoria's cousin, Field Marshal HRH The Duke of Cambridge, the youngest divisional infantry commander to have participated at Balaclava in October 1854.

So the legend has it, a grand celebration parade was held to mark the end of the war. Bands assembled from many regiments to play the national anthem as a grand finale. But so disastrous was the per-formance that the Duke set about creating a training school for army musicians. Queen Victoria later afforded the 'Royal' attaching the School of Military Music.

'The Return of all Persons who Slept or Abode in the Royal Musical School' on Census Night 1891 was carried out by the Commandant, Colonel Thomas Bradney Shaw-Hillier whose personal domestic staff included a cook, an upper housemaid and an under housemaid. Adjutant Frederick Henry Mahoney, as the Captain Quartermaster also resided at the Hall with his wife, son and two daughters and with call on their own general domestic servant celebrating in the name of Sarah Squelsh. The only other married incumbents were Sergeants Carr and Whitear. Otherwise 18 other NCOs and 135 Private soldiers occupied the Hall.

Colonel Francis Bennington-Foote, Chief Resident of the Institution, carried out the Return for 1901. After himself as the Head of the Household, was his wife Agnes and four domestic servants. Adjutant Frederick Henry Mahoney was still in post, but with no mention of his wife, his son and his two daughters, only a housekeeper. Otherwise, the school accommodated 24 NCOs and 129 Private soldiers, mostly under the age of 19, each roundly audited as 'Boy'. With echoes of empire colliding with a poverty-ridden homeland, nine of these boys were born in India and 13 did not know where they were born.

As census enumerator, Mr Giltrow was supposed to note all Institutions including churches, schools, orphanages and business premises, but for some reason failed to add Kneller Hall. Instead he included the second Lodge, which, as with the first, lay within the jurisdiction of the War Department. Pictured central to this view (c.1905) it survives largely unchanged as the guard house.

Here 37-year-old Staff Sergeant Francis Hawkin headed the household in 1901. A British subject born in India, he returned to the mother country sometime before 1887 when he married Chatham girl, Margaret. A year later their first child, William, was born in Southsea, Hampshire. William's younger sister and two brothers were all born in Whitton where the family was posted in 1892. Remarkably, considering his rank, Francis Hawkin could afford to maintain a domestic servant, 17-year-old local girl, Annie Young.

When Mr Giltrow called by, a reasonably sized detached house sat beneath the thick canopy of trees (right), known as The Croft. The same house is recorded in the 1891 census as Woodward Cottage, where market garden employer Arthur Woodward had moved in 1885 with his wife, Eliza, their four children, Arthur's father and one domestic servant, 18-year-old Frances Martin.

By 1901 the Woodwards had moved on, leaving members of another prominent market gardening dynasty to occupy the house and change its name to The Croft. The Manns family had been established in Whitton since the 1870s and would continue to run their substantial business well into the 1920s.

Mr Giltrow records 66 year old Charlotte Mann as living on her own means in The Croft together with her 40-year-old unmarried daughter, also called Charlotte, and her 20 year-old brother Frederick, who was born in Whitton. Frederick's occupation is given as market gardener but not on his own account at this stage in his career. Twenty-one year old Mary Wiltshire was scheduled on Census Night as their domestic servant.

As it had once been for Catholics, so this quarter of Whitton was at the turn of the 20th century one favoured by market garden employers. Immediately west of The Croft towards Whitton village was Kneller Cottage, once the home of George Higgs who came to Whitton from Fulham before 1861 as an unmarried 26 year-old. Accompanying him was his younger brother Richard, his housekeeper, Ann Rudduck, and Labourers Jane and Joseph Ruddock, an aunt and a cousin respectively. George Higgs married Caroline in 1866 and went on to have three daughters, Caroline, Louisa and Emelia. He married again sometime before 1872 and had five more children by his new wife, Ann.

After his death in 1886, Frank Peacock, a highly successful market gardener from Turnham Green took over the business and moved into Kneller Cottage along with his wife, Annie and their six children. Ernest, the youngest being born there. Within a short space of time Frank Peacock had extended the business beyond Whitton towards Hounslow and Isleworth and had become one of the highest taxpayers in the district plus £284 a year in rent and £34 rates for the house in Kneller Road, with 164 acres of arable and orchard land as far afield as Percy Road and Hospital Bridge Road. Part of Frank Peacock's holdings included the ground that would in 1906 be turned over to the Rugby Football Union as the site for their new stadium.

Many residents in the district remember the greengrocery shops run by the Peacock family until the 1970s, but none the sight and smell of the pig farm behind Kneller Cottage, or when the open land following the course of Nelson Road was made available to play cricket and used for the summer fair. Frank Peacock is pictured below, third from the right.

Warren Road to the south was built in 1931 as the main thoroughfare from Twickenham to the new town of Whitton. Thirty years later and the junction with Hounslow Road had become so heavily overloaded that a case was made to provide a direct route by straightening the twin meanders of Kneller Road and cutting through the heart of the village. Kneller Cottage and The Croft were cleared before the scheme was abandoned.

The alignment of this ill-fated scheme is marked by a terrace of distinctly 1960s townhouses angled from The Duke of Cambridge beer garden to where the new Day Centre awaits a new use. Another casualty of this 60s blight was the Old School, which, for half a century, represented Whitton's single access to education.

In 1648 provision was made for a mixed school in the parish of Twickenham, which included Whitton. Between 1686 and 1699 a schoolmaster was appointed with an allowance made for three poor boys to attend free of charge. Later a free, or charity, school was set up in Twickenham, which had become much neglected until 1749 when it was revived and a schoolmaster appointed who was forbidden to take private pupils. From 1750 ten of the pupils were boarded, all were given clothes, but they were expected to pay their way making nets and pins, or picking oakum, a painful and mind-numbing task also performed by workhouse inmates and as a punishment for Naval prisoners, who were required to pick two pounds of tarred rope every day to be used for packing seams and caulking.

As well as the schoolmaster receiving the profits of his living, the boys were forcibly apprenticed when they left as one of the chief ends of the charity. Twenty boys attended the school until 1785 when the number was raised to 30. A school for girls was started in Twickenham in 1717 with most of the income coming from subscriptions and later a few small endowments from legacies. In 1776 there were 24 girls attending. All were given clothes, taught to read and write and how to become 'common servants'.

In 1833 Anglican and Roman Catholic Church schools received a small grant from the government to create what were known as National Schools. However, the opportunities they provided for children of the working poor to learn much above the absolute basics was extremely limited. One teacher might be in charge of 200 children and the average leaving age was 10 years. By 1840 there were twenty schools in Twickenham parish, including an infant school, with around 300 children in attendance. Although some children from Whitton would have had access to education by this time, the greater opportunity presented itself after 1842 with the opening of Archdeacon Cambridge School, just a two-mile walk from Whitton village.

On 11 May 1853, Whitton was provided with St Philip and St James' School, 'to be for ever appropriated and used as a school for the education of children and adults, or children only of the labouring, manufacturing and other poorer classes of the District'. Governance was declared under the Principal Officiating Minister of Holy Trinity and the Principal of the ill-fated Training School at Kneller Hall with 'absolute power of appointment and dismissal of any master or mistress of the school and their assistants'.

The Schools, Whitton. W.H.A 2541.

By the time of Mr Giltrow's enumeration, Whitton had been a separate ecclesiastical parish for less than 30 years and any jurisdiction over the school by the vicar of Holy Trinity was virtually extinct. For all but four years of the deed, the War Department had superseded the requirements of the previous institution.

The school building itself fronting onto Kneller Road was 'fairly well built with red brick facings, stone dressings and slated roofs... closely bounded by the grounds of Kneller Hall on the north and east....fairly well lighted and ventilated on the south and west sides and heated by means of open fireplaces'. The height of the rooms and the size of classrooms were considered to be satisfactory.

The Code of Regulations governing the curriculum laid down that the children were taught reading, writing and arithmetic, as well as needlework, drawing, singing and physical exercise. The playground was deemed to be of 'insufficient size and neither paved nor drained'.

The only physical evidence that school ever existed is in the change to the brickwork in the wall bounding Kneller Hall along Kneller Road and Whitton Dene, or Whitton Dean, as this historically ambiguous quarter separating Whitton and Isleworth was known before the 1930s. Past chroniclers of Whitton's history have traditionally included the impressive Queen Anne mansion known as The Manor House in its annals. Never actually a Manor House as such, this fine building lost to development in the 1930s more correctly belongs to the history of Heston & Isleworth (now the London Borough of Hounslow) and was therefore excluded from Mr Giltrow's enumeration.

Just out of view to the left of The Manor House towards Whitton village is the borderline between both parishes. Whitton Dean Farm sat on the Twickenham side. A document dated 1439 refers to a long standing 'debate and strif' since before the time of Domesday, which settled where this boundary lay according to the course of Birket's Brook. Until 1935, the brook was still an open stream, which flowed into the grounds of Kneller Hall to feed the ornamental lake. The last of the otters living along the banks of Birket's Brook were hunted to extinction as late as 1898.

A partially drowned Alexander Pope was carried from this spot to Nathaniel Pigott's house after being thrown from his carriage into the swollen river. The 'ancient bridge' he fell foul of was at the time of Mr Giltrow's enumeration a stone slab fording a modest ditch.

Arthur Woodward was running Whitton Dean Farm in 1901, his offspring by now doubled to eight and with only his father having failed to survive the move from Woodward Cottage. Complete with its own orchard and grazing to the rear (now Murray Park) and north into Whitton Dean, and with two acres to the south towards the village, local people collected their milk daily from Whitton Dean Farm in domestic canisters deep into the 20th century. The better off had it delivered.

Returning to Kneller Road and Whitton village, Mr Giltrow's view south and to the east of Nelson Road was largely of uninterrupted countryside. Only the Red Lion public house jutted out onto the roadside. The Market Place didn't come about until in 1906, with its modest array of Edwardian shops largely unchanged. The oddly shaped Triangle Café immediately north of them was originally a chemist, complete with a glazed roof to provide natural light for the photographer's studio.

The house of Georgian appearance on the west side of Nelson Road (right) represents the oldest domestic dwelling in Whitton. Originally built as four shops after 1895, 1 – 4 Clarence Terrace (below) is today 112 – 188 Kneller Road.

Occupying the corner of Kneller Road and Whitton Dean was 1, Clarence Terrace where Mr Giltrow recorded Elizabeth Allenson as the head of the household with two of her four rooms given over to lodgers, Harry A. Hackle, a market garden labourer, his wife Emily and their one-year-old daughter also called Emily.

In number two, with no room for them at the Married Quarters, were billeted student bandsman William Gibson, his wife, two sons and a nephew. Sixty-five-year-old Maria Elliot was living on her own means at number three and in number four was Walter Lewis, his wife Frances and their three children. Declaring his occupation as that of a grocer's assistant it is likely that Walter was employed next door in the store where his near neighbour, Elizabeth Allenson was born.

The grocery store was a good-sized house already of some age when James Allenson started his grocery business there in 1848, the year he probably added the front store extension. As well as an agent for the Atlas Fire and Life Assurance Company, James Allenson also established Whitton's first Post Office in the days when the London mail coach arrived for collection at 7.45 am and 2.45 pm, with the west bound collection and delivery at 8 am and 3 pm.

All other post office business such as the purchase of postal orders could only be conducted at the main post offices in Richmond and Hounslow. Otherwise, the day-to-day business of Allenson's store was much as we recognise it today with the demise of main post offices in favour of sub-post offices often sited in convenience stores. Whereas nowadays these outlets are imbued with the aroma of everything from soap powder, sweets and newspaper, when James Allenson died in 1863, coffee, cocoa and exotic fruits such as lemons and oranges; nuts, spices and blocks of chocolate were all becoming available.

Matches were sold in boxes or upright tins. Sugar was cut from a solid cone or 'loaf' into required weights. Salt came in a block, and soap was a slab eighteen inches long, which was sliced into one-pound bars. Everything was wrapped in paper; blue for sugar, yellow for dried fruit and white or brown for other goods.

By 1881 Mrs Allenson had been running the business for 18 years, possibly assisted by Elizabeth who was then aged 35, unmarried and declaring no occupation. Her younger sister Mary had married Professor of Music, Robert Martin, and had three children, Ernest aged three, Clarence aged one and Sidney of four months.

The major innovation in retailing by this time was the emergence of branded goods. As well as Huntley & Palmer and Peak Frean's biscuits, Horniman's packaged their tea, which for the first time guaranteed quality. In blending their own, many an unprincipled grocer devised all manner of underhand schemes such as adding cheaper ingredients to their own blends to increase the volume.

Before the Adulteration of Food Act in 1860, water was commonly patted into slabs of butter. Umber, or red earth, was mixed with cocoa. Beer and milk was watered down and alum added to flour. Tougher measures to crack down on this abuse were introduced in 1872 and 1875. By 1891 when most local authorities had appointed inspectors and food analysts to enforce these laws, Mrs Allenson and her daughter had quit the grocery business and transferred the Post Office to the newly built shop on the corner of Kneller Road and Whitton Dean.

Between then and Mr Giltrow's enumeration, Mrs Allenson had died and the Post Office had moved to the south side of the village. Her daughter was now aged 55, unmarried and reduced to taking in lodgers. At her former home entered next by Mr Giltrow simply as 'Shop' the head of the household was Thomas Goldsmith, an agricultural labourer from Sussex. His wife, Harriet, was recorded as shopkeeper working on her own account.

Even during those unenlightened times with regard to the role and position of women in society, Harriet's occupation placed her far higher up the social scale than that of her husband. Her contribution to the household income far exceeded that of her spouse in volume and regularity. Like today's convenience stores, she traded until 8 pm on weekdays and on Saturdays as late as 11 pm, when she would have taken well over half the weekly income.

Elizabeth Allenson would hold the lease of the building until six months after the census of 1911 when the Medical Officer of Health would describe 'the dwelling house...previously used as The Old Post Office' to be 'in such a bad state as to be unfit for human habitation'. In a subsequent letter, the Health, Bathing and Allotment Committee would learn that the owner of the premises was 'dangerously ill' and that the news of a closing order being made on her property might have dire effects'.

However, the proposal to let the matter rest would be challenged by the Town Clerk, leading the owner's representative to attempt to ascertain what could be done to render the building habitable. But in accordance with the Housing and Town Planning Act 1909, it would be deemed beyond repair. The failure to appeal against demolition within 21 days and the owner not having taken down and removed the buildings within three months automatically authorised the borough Surveyor to do so. The costs were covered by the sale of materials, with the balance of any proceeds thereafter going to the owner. Thus on 18 November 1912 was lost one of Whitton's oldest and most characterful buildings. It is now the site of Whitton Scrap.

Across the road from the shop were the four artisan cottages adjacent to The White Hart public House we see today and which managed to survive a similar fate. What is today number 113, Kneller Road was in 1901 number four White Hart Cottages, occupied by William Spindler, a market garden labourer from Berkshire who came to Whitton with his wife Harriet in 1886 and had subsequently filled their four-roomed accommodation with seven children. Next door at number three, Mr Giltrow found William Garwood, a solider in the 1st Suffolk Regiment who married Hounslow Girl, Nellie, five or six years earlier and whose three children were also born in the area.

Today we can only imagine the living conditions endured by some of some the poorest households visited by Mr Giltrow. While there were commitments on the part of local authorities to remedy the often-appalling living conditions prevalent amongst working families and to overcome their exploitation by unscrupulous landlords, the question of personal hygiene was by no means necessarily rooted there. What is regarded as unacceptable nowadays was often the standard a century ago based on traditional values and ignorance.

The whole question of public health has its origins in a report by social reformer Edwin Chadwick published in 1842. With the spectre of cholera rife in the slums, he concluded that the most important measures that could be taken to improve the health of the public were drainage, the removal of refuse from houses, streets and roads and the improvements of water supplies. Such was the drive to educate and eradicate the fundamental lack of knowledge about hygiene that departments of public health were established in every local government district with a Medical Health Officer taking control of the environment. The Inspector of Nuisances was charged with reporting to the Health Committee all breaches of the byelaws and regulations constituting a nuisance.

Both engineer labourer Edwin Meacock occupying 2, White Hart Cottages and his immediate neighbour, William Garwood at number three would find themselves entered into the Journal and Diary of the Medical Health Officer who described their living conditions as being 'dirty and unwholesome', with the properties requiring whitewashing and a cleansing order. Twickenham born, Harry Harris and his wife Annie from Dorset were living at number one. As a carpenter and joiner, Harry would have known well the man living directly opposite in the more impressive house bearing the name of the family who formerly owned all the land hereabouts.

Gostling House was an ornate, double fronted dwelling from where blacksmith, builder, undertaker and entrepreneur, James Wills, controlled his modest business empire. He probably changed the name of the house from The Cottage after 1891 when, as a 31-year-old carpenter he was living there with his wife Elizabeth and their four children. Despite that number of offspring grown to six by 1901, the family lived in luxury compared to the conditions of their immediate neighbours. In 1913 James Wills would be first elected to the Twickenham Urban District Council. A year later, and mindful of the approaching urbanisation of Whitton, he would go on to secure the old pleasure ground behind his house as a Park for the People to be called Murray Park in honour of Colonel Gostling-Murray, the last of Whitton's landed elite.

The ornate frontage of Gostling House is just visible to the right of the bus passing through Kneller Road in this photograph taken in the 1920s. Between it and the gap left by the demolition of the old Post Office are Post Office Cottages, which were in 1901 jointly occupied by John Glenister, a 35-year-old agricultural labourer from Buckinghamshire, his wife Sarah and their seven children. Typical of the times, the bulging Glenister household also found room for a little extra income in the form of boarder, George Edy, a 30-year-old farm labourer from Sussex.

Malcolm Young, a 45-year-old Whitton-born market garden fore-man, his wife Sarah and their three-year old son Reuben occupied two rooms in one of these cottages and farm carter, James Rogers and his wife, Elizabeth the other two. To the far side of Gostling House were Hyde's Cottages and Hyde's Cottage, all of which, including Gostling House and Post Office Cottages have been replaced by the Tudorbethan-style parade of shops and inter-war houses we see today.

Agricultural labourer Charles Ayliff from Hampshire had been living in Hyde's Cottages since before 1881 with his wife, Catherine. One of the four rooms they were occupying in 1901 was rented out to lodger, Samuel Cox, an agricultural worker also from Hampshire. Edwin and Jemima Francis next door declared the same occupation. Hyde's Cottage was where blacksmith Harry Greenbank, his wife Lena, their three children and Lodger Frederick Coombs were living in 1891. Harry was Yorkshireman born in Bradford. His first son Harold was born in Warburton, Hampshire in 1886, and daughter Lena was born in Hounslow a year later. The Greenbanks arrived in Whitton in 1890 where Frank, the youngest son, was born.

Harry's wife, also called Lena, was born in Bethnal Green in 1863 and appears on the 1891 census for Whitton as a Farrier and General Smith, one of 347 female blacksmiths working in Britain at that time. If not fully-fledged, then Lena Greenbank may well have ranked amongst the 9,000 other women smiths making nails for horseshoes. No woman would normally have been accepted as an apprentice or employee into such a trade, although wives' involvement in the family business was by no means unusual. Often they took over in the event of their husbands' death. By this means, women became the proprietors of many trades otherwise considered unsuitable for their sex. Women often ran such businesses successfully and, in some cases, expanded them as they prospered.

Conversely, the likes of Susannah Hyde declared no profession or occupation. As befitting his trade as a carpenter & wheelwright, John Hyde was able to afford his wife's complete attention to the more superior home they shared with 16-year-old apprentice Harold Weston. Village artisans and tradesmen such as he were the aristocrats of labour in the parish. As such their wives were not so concerned with earning extra income, as were other women less fortunate than themselves. As for Lena Greenbank, she had by 1901 acquired both an eighth child, a more respectable place of birth (Havant, Hertfordshire) and declared no occupation, thus suggesting an elevation in her social standing commensurate with the Edwardian middle class ideal.

The White Hart Inn on the south side of Kneller Road was in 1635 a cottage occupied by John Smallhouse. A Survey of Middlesex public houses in 1685 is thought to refer to this premises with three bedrooms for hire and stabling for 12 horses. However, in a will dated 4th November 1688, Yeoman Henry Pavett bequeathed the cottage to his wife, Jane, along with barns, an orchard and gardens with no mention of it being used as an alehouse or Inn. It is not until 1727 that we find the premises first advertised by John Underwood of Twickenham as The White Hart Ale House. Admitted as tenants in 1869 were John and Henry Sich, a name that remained over the door when Inn Keeper, John Butler, was landlord in 1901.

As Whitton's oldest surviving commercial premises, what we see today includes elements of the building dating back to the 17th century. The 'wings' either side of the original structure are later additions. The east wing probably dates to the 18th century when a chaisehouse was added. It was used until the 1980s as an off-licence and liquor store. Then a passage running beneath the hayloft led to one of two public bars and through to the rear garden. The hayloft above survives.

In 1901, the entrance to the main public bar was via a door central to the front bay, today replaced by a window. To the right of that was a lounge measuring ten foot by eight foot with a small round table in the middle and chairs placed all around the walls. Despite its cramped conditions this space was used for public meetings and the election of local councillors. The photograph below was taken in 1906 when Chinese slavery in the Transvaal was an issue for the Liberal government.

By the time of Mr Giltrow's enumeration, the Hydes had left Whitton and the Greenbanks, as Farriers and Wheelwrights, had moved to The Forge next door (pictured right). Harold, the eldest son at age 14, was working as an apprentice to his father. There had been a Forge on this site since at least 1789 when Jeremiah Murden owned it and the fields to the west. A car showroom now occupies the site, which is still referred to by some locals as 'Field's Garage', a name carried down the years since the establishment of Whitton's first motor garage after 1918. Members of the same family manned its pumps until the tiny service station closed in 1989. Well within living memory local people called here to have red hot iron forged into farm and gardening implements, or to mend a domestic iron pot.

Hyde's Cottages opposite The Forge (pictured below) were recorded by Mr Giltrow as numbers one and two Edith Cottages. Number
one was probably none too savoury when Mr Giltrow called, as a
later Inspector of Nuisances report made plain.

Describing the dwelling as 'very dilapidated' with 'severe defects', the recommended visit to be paid by the Medical Health Officer was undertaken 14 days later when the 'unwholesome' abode was found to be in such a dilapidated state that it was in his opinion 'injurious and a nuisance to health'. Charles Aldridge, a builder's labourer, had been living there since 1895 when he and his wife, Hannah, arrived in Whitton and where their first child, William, was born. With two other sons and one daughter, they shared their four-roomed accommodation with boarder, Jesse Brown, a garden labourer, born in Whitton.

Alfred Mack, a general labourer from Isleworth was living in number two with his wife Sarah, their three children and a niece. Subsequently replaced by numbers 138 and 140 Kneller Road, these cottages represented the final frontier of domestic occupation along the entire north side of Kneller Road as far as Hounslow Road. Until 1901 the Forge was the last building on the south side before the church and its associated buildings, except for a new development of four Villas under way along this stretch set out before a gated exotic-filled arboretum, which is now Murray Park.

Only one of numbers 1-4 Kneller Villas (now 165 – 171 Kneller Road) was inhabited at the time of Mr Giltrow's enumeration. Two were found to have fallen below the quality required under the local byelaws in that the mortar used was so poor that notice was served on the builder to tear them down and rebuild. Although planning permission as such didn't exist at this time, building regulations were if anything stricter than they sometimes appear to be now. Builders were required to buy a sixpenny guide to regulations and were expected to comply fully with the council's expectations, to remedy sub-standard work and demolish unauthorised structures.

Otherwise, these new developments expressed a continuation of the middle class aspirational flight from London that was starting to attract speculative builders to areas of prime development potential, such as Whitton.

NELLER RD. WHITTON.

50

Such dwellings would eventually be on offer for three pounds down and ten shillings a year instalments without interest. No taxes, no tithes, free conveyances and even free roads and improvements added to the attraction of owning a part of Whitton Park Estate in which to enjoy 'absolute quiet and seclusion within 29 minutes of London's centre.'

Kneller Villas also represented the first in Whitton of a new style of housing indicative of the Edwardian era, displaying a period of revivalism, mixing and matching many influences including the medieval. In architectural terms, the Edwardian period was from 1901 through to 1918, taking inspiration from the Arts and Crafts movement and encompassing a fresh look at vernacular traditions beyond the often-dour Victorian confections towards the more organic Art Nouveau influences in stained glass, door furniture and wider frontages. A number of these themes are expressed in these Villas in their roughcast walls, archetypal Tudor style wood and render treatment of gable and facing walls called black and white, or magpie-work. Jacobean details could also include mullioned windows, Dutch gables and large bays with sash windows.

Pure Arts and Crafts products were too expensive and not available in sufficient quantity, so many building products were machine-made. The 'Tudorbethan' look, sometimes called the 'Quaint' style, first appeared from the late 1890s, was scorned by 1910, but persists to the present day. Other examples are also apparent on Kneller Road in the form of local authority housing, built more than 20 years after Mr Giltrow's enumeration when growth in Britain after the First World War was particularly concentrated in the Greater London area. Four years of conflict, the high costs of raw materials and rent control, gave rise to the Tudor Walters Report of 1918, which set out to assuage the poor quality housing endured by the working classes. The Garden City Movement and primarily the Addison Acts of 1919 drove housing legislation in a celebration of design, landscaping and density of working class housing. Those examples facing Kneller Road demonstrate an especially high quality, well-planned development within a pleasant suburban setting, well appointed with a view of uninterrupted countryside when they were built.

Glimpsed behind the fencing to the left of this view, their aspect from the roadside was as important a statement of municipal intent as the motivation behind them was directly influenced by post-war changes in economic and social policy it brought about. Other examples less well situated along Kneller Road, in Colonial Avenue, Cedar Avenue and Prospect Crescent are less exuberant in their design.

While the housing of Whitton's working classes was on the wider agenda in 1901, it was not yet a priority. The break up of Whitton Park opened the door for those who could afford to possess their own piece of English history at no cost to the ratepayer. The first of these pioneer settlers was 64-year-old widow Hannah Edward from Cornwall, newly settled in number four Kneller Villas, now 165 Kneller Road.

Scheduled as 'Lame' in the appropriate column of Mr Giltrow's schedule, Mrs Edward was by profession a poultry rearer, working at home on her own account. Perhaps forsaking marriage to care for her invalid mother was 35-year-old daughter Rhoda, also born in Cornwall and working as a mantle maker, a highly tailored item of women's clothing worn over a dress. Mother and daughter would have enjoyed their situation as befitting the quintessential rural idyll contained in the estate agents' literature.

The village was near enough to walk to and far enough away to ensure peace and privacy, and with the church comfortably close for regular attendance. The view from the rear of the new house was of fields and orchards peppered with red-roofed cottages and the occasional black-slated villa punctuating clutches of venerable exotic and native trees.

To the front was open countryside glimpsed through a tight forest of cedar, oak, beech, sweet chestnut, acacia, Holm oak and other rare and fine specimens, some planted in the 1730s by Lord Ilay, later Third Duke of Argyle, when he built the Whitton Dean Estate for his mistress, Mrs Elizabeth Anne Williams and their two illegitimate children. Then it boasted a fine Palladian villa complete with offices, orangery and stables for 12 horses. What remained when Mr Giltrow called by was a large lake set beside the stables off Whitton Dean. The Old Riding School, otherwise known as The Drill Hall (pictured below to the right of the house) was replaced by Murray Park Community Hall in 1935 and is the only physical reference point surviving this lost estate.

Whitton Dean near Hounslow belonging to Mrs Campbell 1791.

Close by in 1901 was a small cottage where Mr Giltrow found John Woolgar, a 57-year-old local born plumber, his wife Selina and their three children, 16-year-old Alfred, a soap boiler by profession, 14-year-old John who worked as an errand boy, nine-year-old Alice and two month old William. The last proper caretakers of the former estate were recorded in 1891 as James and Caroline Silwood. Ten years later and with the whole of the Whitton Park Estate being sold up, this portion had acquired the name of The Fairmead Estate.

From the existing eastern border of Murray Park, Fairmead Estate extended as far as the rear gardens on the west side of Colonial Avenue, Old Whitton's first new road since medieval times. Up for auction on 6th June 1901 were 15 freehold building plots at a point along Whitton Dean Road to the north and 12 more due south on Kneller Road. This reduced the estate by 335 feet, leaving the 10.5 acres James Wills would manage to save as a Park for The People in 1914. When Whitton Dene (as it then became called) was widened in 1935, the old estate boundary wall and stable block were torn down. The ornamental lake was filled in and the Drill Hall made way for the Community Hall glimpsed below to the left of this 1960s view of Murray Park looking north towards Whitton Dene.

Murray Park, Whitton.

By rights the new pleasure ground should have carried the name of councillor James Wills, the man who saved it for the people of Whitton for all time. But it was decided in a final act of deference to name it after the last of the local gentry who in 1850 had married the niece of the two sisters who owned Whitton Park and where the whole family moved in 1854. When his wife died in 1859 after the birth of their sixth child, followed two months later by one of the sisters, Charles Edward Murray became the head of the estate, a task he undertook with relish.

In true hierarchical style, the picturesque former pleasure grounds were opened up for a variety of annual events including the Holy Trinity Church Sunday Schools outing where the children would assemble behind their banner and the band of the 4th Royal South West Middlesex Militia for the procession from Hounslow to the Drill Ground. The Peoples' Great Holiday Festival was the annual rural fete organised by the Committee of the Hounslow Working Men's Club held on Whit-Monday since 1859 with 'excellent and powerful' entertainment provided by military bands, 'popular and charismatic comedians', stars of Music Hall, Olympic games, rustic sports, archery and cricket, broadsword, foils and singlestick, a circus, rifle gallery and dancing on The Green.

In May that same year, public anxiety over the possibility of French aggression led Lord Derby's Government to authorise the formation of Volunteer Rifle Corps throughout the land. The 16th South West Rifles were formed of four companies; No.1 Twickenham, Whitton, No.2 Brentford, No.3 Hounslow, Heston and No.4 Isleworth, Feltham. Charles Edward Murray was made Captain of the local company and later Colonel of the rifle regiment. But who were the 16th South West Middlesex Volunteers, asked a reporter from the Middlesex Chronicle. "How were they organised? How did you get in?"

Only recruits whose character bore the closest, the strictest enquiry and were known to two of the old members and with nothing found against their respectability were allowed to join the ranks. And no recruit left his squad until he passed an examination. In August 1870, the 16th South West Middlesex, or 'Ours', as the *Middlesex Chronicle* preferred to call them, paraded at the Brighton Volunteer Military Review where they first formed into a square to resist a cavalry charge, then deployment, skirmishing, file firing, volley firing and a bayonet charge. Later they marched past in quick and double time and did manual exercises under the senior Major. The arms and accoutrements of every man were minutely examined before wheeling into line to receive Inspection with a general salute. On their return home, the men fell in on the platform of the Whitton Park railway station (now Hounslow) and headed by two bands, the 477 men (50 more than the previous year) marched down Whitton Road towards the Drill Ground.

"Oh, the shame of it all!" cried the Chronicle's reporter with one or two ineffectual officer voices and some dirty rifles marring the impressive sight and sound of the spectacle. "Especially with Colonel Murray of Whitton Park as commanding officer", who in a sure and clear voice reminded the men that "with Prussia and France at war, we cannot be sure how long we will be neutral". Pondering on that thought, all ranks then went to a secluded part of the park grounds for refreshment before the band led the battalion back to the railway station for dismissal. "Whitton," the Chronicle reported, "your glory will live forever".

Colonel Murray had turned the old Riding School into a drill hall, deploying musketry instructor John Thompson and his wife Elizabeth and son Richard in the small cottage close by. Here was established the headquarters of the local regiment and where the men were drilled 'in the noble arts of warfare'. For a while the north wall of the drill hall was used for target practice. Later, the rifle butts (pictured overleaf) were set up in the northeast corner of the ground to save the 18th century structure from slow erosion.

"It was Dr Sydenham," reported *The Richmond & Twickenham Times* "who said that the holding of a rural fete in a town is more beneficial to the health than a cart loaded with medicine", which was just as well, as medicine and medical care for most of the attendees was hard to come by. An assistant surgeon, Thomas Wright Fenwick, was living in Whitton in 1881. In 1901, Charles Aspray, Doctor of Medicine, was occupying Vicarage Cottage in Kneller Road.

Charles Aspray may well have practised at Twickenham's Cottage Hospital where he might have given of his services free to the most destitute, or seen to it that the fees paid were reimbursed, which still meant even the most impoverished finding the money in the first place. While the value of the preventative nature of the Medical Health Officer's work was immeasurable, health care in post-Victorian Britain was a luxury few could afford. Hospitals were typically simple affairs for the poor, run on a largely voluntary basis with a minimum of staff catering for a huge range of ailments and injuries from haemorrhoids to cancer.

Elizabeth Twining, one of nine children born to Richard Twining, the tea merchant, promoted many philanthropic and educational schemes in Twickenham, including the founding of St. John's Hospital. Prospective patients, however, had to be recommended by the governors of the hospital Trust and to make a contribution of five shillings per week towards their care, a substantial amount of money, so for the most part the working poor and lower middle classes went without medical treatment, relying instead on dubious and sometimes dangerous home remedies.

Some dentition care was available at Cottage Hospitals like St John's, but again care was mostly confined to prevention. Brown bread was thought to keep teeth clean. Chewing tough celery acted like dental floss and soot mixed with salt rubbed onto the teeth was a popular formula for toothpaste. For the better off in 1901 there were trained and licensed dental surgeons providing operations using efficient electric rotary drills. But for the vast majority of the population extraction was the only cure for a troublesome tooth, and without the benefit of the new nitrous-oxide gas or cocaine.

Professional examinations in optometry had been around for six years before Mr Giltrow's enumeration, with the formation of the British Optical Association in 1895. Until then, jewellers and watchmakers produced spectacles for those that could afford them. Grim Asylum institutions such as Normansfield in neighbouring Teddington (now a gated housing estate) provided for the mentally ill. The old who were incapable of looking after themselves often ended their days in the Brentford Union workhouse (now The West Middlesex Hospital) where paupers did unpaid work in return for food and shelter well into the 20th century.

Vicarage Cottage, where Doctor Aspray lived, stood immediately east of the Vicarage, then the very antithesis of the featureless box currently planted in the remnants of once substantial grounds. Vicarage Cottage was situated off the highway towards the rear of a wedge of land fronted by what are now numbers 195 and 199 Kneller Road. Joseph Messenger lived there as the parish clerk in 1891 and before him, Frank Holding, an accountant and debt-collector. Having secured the details of Charles Aspray, his wife, Christine, and son Charlie, a 30-year-old surveyor born in Paddington, John Burridge Giltrow rounded the corner of Vicarage Road to call on what was before the 1960s despoliation, a splendidly ornate Victorian Gothic pile built shortly after the church of St Philip and St James was consecrated in 1862. Half its grounds were sold off a century later to make way for White Farm Lodge, a local authority rest home, itself recently torn down to make way for a larger 'partnership' version of the same.

The Reverend George C Robinson was enjoying the Whitton living before 1901, together with his wife, Maria, their 27-year-old son, Stephen and daughter Mildred. Two domestic servants, Emma Green and Mary Hill catered for the Robinsons' needs. Stephen Robinson had taken up an interesting occupation for a Victorian vicar's son, that of actor, an ambition still high on the list of disreputable professions. However, this was the age of the great actor managers such as Sir Henry Beebohn Tree, presenting his realistic productions and lavish sets at Her Majesty's Theatre in London, and Sir Henry Irving, the most celebrated Englishman of his time, playing Coriolanus at the Lyceum.

Irving's knighthood in 1895 was the first bestowed upon an actor, making a life on the boards almost respectable. The Richmond Theatre and Opera House opened in 1899 with a performance of Shakespeare's As You Like It. Twickenham's first Town Hall incorporated an auditorium (known today as the Queen's Hall) where Lillie Langtry made her debut in 1881. Music Hall had begun in the 1850s as largely a working class entertainment with its roots in beer halls and gin palaces. Initially shunned by polite society, it had grown in popularity and respectability. The large, open halls set out with tables and chairs had by the turn of the 20th century largely given way to that of drink-free, theatrical auditoria ideally suited for the new form of popular mass entertainment that many a serious actor initially despised.

Britain was quick to embrace the cinema with its first exhibition having taken place in 1896. The potential of film as a conveyor of news and particularly sport was soon established and moving pictures of music hall acts, trick and comedy films and dramatic stories were being shown anywhere a screen could be set up, benches laid out and money taken. *Stop Thief* produced in 1901 was an early example of the 'chase movie,' defining the techniques and grammar of film editing and narrative continuity.

Whitton was graced with The Ritz in the 1930s, which stood opposite the Admiral Nelson in the new High Street. It later formed part of the Odeon chain and survived for 30 years before making way for flats and offices. The old Town Hall in King Street, Twickenham, first served to put on local film shows until the first permanent cinema was built in the town, the 300-seat Twickenham Picture Palace in King Street, which operated from 1910 to 1914.

By 1901, the days of pageants, plays and the other wholesome entertainments once provided by Colonel Murray were well and truly over. The main source of respectable community activity in Whitton was provided as elsewhere by the local church as a sop to the mainstay of the most popular form of entertainment of all, drink. Horace Walpole records 18th century Whitton as being 'a resort of characters not of the best class'. He writes of a robbery by a footpad at one-o'clock in the afternoon, and one knight of the road...'having attained unenviable celebrity, lay in state in Whitton'. Indeed, the land provided for the church of St Philip and St James was such a violent and lawless resort for 'tipplers, swearers, and all sorts of vagabonds' that it gave rise to a most unlikely saviour who unleashed on the offenders a rigorous blend of philanthropic social control.

Louis Kyezor was a successful Jewish businessman who first came to Whitton in about 1839 and almost immediately became active across a host of charitable and municipal works with the avowed intent of improving the hamlet, 'notorious as a nest of ruffians' and to eradicate its 'dirt, sensuality, irreligion, and ignorance'. Not a man to be trifled with, Kyezor went about his business with a pair of flintlock pistols tucked into his belt as he drew attention to 'the want of a place of worship' for the 'heathen village'. The worst elements of the neighbourhood were encouraged to emigrate, while work was found for their children and houses provided for the poorest classes. Having galvanised popular support, Kyezor secured for Whitton an identity of its own, with the wider community finally enjoying their fair share of the Twickenham Charities and the wealthy a new order.

The foundation stone of 'Whitton church' was laid on 17 July 1861 by Augustus Murray, aged seven, the eldest son of Colonel Murray, on ground given by Miss Maria Gostling who also gave the bell tower surmounted by its elegant stone spirelet. Charles Murray, who had been a member of the Church Committee, gave the chancel and triple east window depicting the life of Christ in memory of his late wife. Constructed of Kentish rag with Bath Stone dressings, St Philip and St James survives much intact in its small haven of tranquillity.

In 1901 there were none of the houses we see today in the vicinity. To the north lay the former Nurserylands and Warren of the Whitton Park Estate. Beyond that were mostly market gardens as far as the London & South West Railway line. To the west of the church across the Hounslow Road was more open land flanked by an ocean of exotic and native trees, testimony to the splendours of Whitton Park where the wealth, indifference and influence of the district's landed elite had rested for the past 150 years, and where John Burridge Giltrow set off for next.

HOUNSLOW ROAD FROM WHITTON PARK
TO HOLLY BUSH CORNER

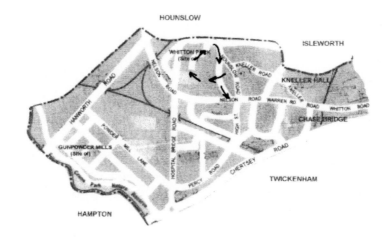

.... *Whitton Park, (not the Lodge in the Hounslow Road),*
then from the Vicarage to the Nelson Inn ....

When Archibald Campbell, Lord Ilay, later Third Duke of Argyll, laid out Whitton Dean for his mistress around 1736 he incorporated an avenue of cedars, uniting both estates. A century and quarter later and the church of St Philip and St James, together with its Vicarage, had rudely interrupted that romantic gesture. Eighty years after that and what remained of the walk west of Hounslow Road was buried beneath the housing we see today. However, by negotiating a strangulated route through predominantly bungalow development after Keswick Road, this section of Mr Giltrow's perambulation can still be roughly echoed.

Runnymede Road and Rydal Gardens striking north from the field attaching Nelson School embrace the site of Argyll's later Palladian villa, which was demolished in the 1850s together with his lover's house at Whitton Dean. The narrow passageway we are required to take today leads to the sole surviving clutch of cedars that today guard the entrance to the Old Latmerians Sports Ground. Opposite here in 1901 stood another of Argyll's civil engineering pursuits in the form of his 40-foot high triangular 'Gothick Tower.'

Built partly for the Duke's astronomic investigations and simply to enjoy the view, the base of this structure persisted as 'Whitton dungeons' until the 1960s when it was used as a store.

Today, only the stout wall to the right of this view survives as one half of a passage between it and a block of maisonettes forming the start of Wills Crescent, ironically named after the councillor who, despite his best efforts, failed to save the park and its features. James Wills was elected chairman of Twickenham Urban District Council in 1925 and later became an Alderman of the new London Borough of Twickenham, comprising the former Urban District Councils of Twickenham (including Whitton), Teddington and The Hamptons. In 1932, he was elected Mayor, but just three days short of his full term office, on 6 November 1933, at the age of 74, he died suddenly. His work for Whitton, his concern for ameliorating poverty and his love of children made him a popular and much admired first citizen.

The arch dug from the mound supporting the tower was originally designed to frame the view of a canal leading to the Duke's greenhouse at the far end represented as a Grecian temple. This waterway was later 'naturalised' into the meandering lake that greeted Mr Giltrow in 1901

Here "the invigorating sport of skating on the charming lake at Whitton Park was kept up with much spirit through the kindness of Colonel Murray". In the 1870s the ice was then "regularly graced with the presence of a number of young ladies, many of who were excellent skaters". On a number of occasions the water was illuminated and fireworks were let off from the top of the ornamental tower. After 1871, admission to the lake for the purpose of skating was by invitation only.

Early filmmakers would re-create jungle scenes here, and in a letter to the Middlesex Chronicle in the late 1960s readers were reminded that a small portion of Whitton Woods still persisted in the form of the headquarters of the 1st Whitton Scout Group. "One original Cedar of Lebanon stands sentinel over 30 or 40 trees of every variety donated and planted in 1964 by supporters of the group. Then this fragment was still used for camping where the boys lit wood fires and cooked sausages as part of their tests.

Today the Kerswell Community and Scout Hall occupies a large chunk of the former lake site, representing what was a hugely unattractive prospect for developers having to fill and prepare such an obstacle.

NEAR HOUNSLOW. THE TOWER, WHITTON WOODS.

Bisecting the Duke's cube-like estate today, Grasmere Avenue leads us snakelike to the site of Argyll's former greenhouse and aviary, afterwards converted into a substantial mansion later known as Whitton Park House.

While all physical references to Whitton Park are lost, the lines of semi-detached houses making up the rest of Wills Crescent form an object lesson in hard landscape archaeology, a built parch mark almost, recording the limit of Argyll's moated estate that took a contingent of 1930s Pioneers months to fill partially with 2,000 tons of imported soil. Fragments of the moat survive in some rear gardens and along the boundary with the Old Latmerians Sports ground.

At 'The Big House' in 1881 the Honourable Charles Edward Gostling-Murray was duly recorded as Hon. Colonel of the 8th Battalion of the West Middlesex Rifle Volunteers Middlesex Volunteers and Justice of the Peace. His second wife, Margaret, 15 years his junior at age 30, was recorded as Wife of a Justice of the Peace, and their one year old son, Farne(?) as the son of a Colonel in the Auxiliary Forces. He was born in London and his four-month-old brother, Cecil, in Whitton. The household staff then comprised a cook, nurse, Lady's maid, two housemaids, a kitchen maid, a nursemaid, a footman and a groom. In March 1891, the Gostling-Murrays were delivered of the last of their children, Gladys, who was born in Whitton like her three-year-old brother, Stracey and one year old sister, Nina. Presumably the two older boys were away at school.

The younger children may have enjoyed one-to-one attention from nurse Louisa Whitfield and the two under nurses, Ellen Firman and Elizabeth Webb, although at this time Colonel Murray was not in the best of health, and possibly they also cared for him. Otherwise, the ailing sole representative of Whitton gentry headed the quintessential upper middle class Victorian household, managed on a day-to-day basis by his wife in accordance with the recognised dictates on domestic economy and household management.

In this, Butler James Eastland was at the top of the domestic ladder, charged with greeting the arrival of guests, looking after the silver and the wine, arranging the dining table and ensuring an efficient household service went unnoticed upstairs. His wife Jane as housekeeper was the most senior member of the female staff. She reported the condition of the household accounts directly to her mistress and advised on the engagement of staff such as 25 year old housemaid Anne Glover from Kent, whose duties mostly involved cleaning all the above stairs rooms, including carpets, walls and ceilings; dusting and washing the china ornaments; looking after the fires and grates, and polishing all the wood and the brass.

Frederick Moss and Joseph Higgins, the two footmen, were responsible for cleaning the cutlery, maintaining and lighting the lamps, waiting at table, ironing newspapers, cleaning boots and shoes and waiting on the gentlemen in the Smoking Room. Emilie Jouvet, suitably imported from France as lady's maid, looked after her mistress's clothes, shoes, jewellery, hair and appearance, often making repairs or alterations; assisting her in dressing and changing, often several times a day, and possibly attending her at engagements and travels with her.

Scottish born Cook Eliza Smail carried the responsibility for all the family meals and those of her fellow servants, agreed each week with the mistress. Eliza's face would have been a familiar one in the community, ordering and arranging for the delivery of all foodstuffs. Like the housekeeper, Mrs Eastland, 54-year-old Eliza Smail selected staff subject to the approval of her employer.

Nineteen-year-old Florence Snowfield from Surrey was starting out in service as scullery maid and 21-year-old Eliza Hymen, also from Surrey, was progressing in hers as kitchen maid. Both would usually be found preparing vegetables, plucking birds, stirring and mixing dishes and an endless round of washing up.

Days for household staff began at 5.30 a.m. Often it would be midnight before they finished. With half a day off a week, they considered themselves lucky compared to the lives of many others outside service. Their positions were highly valued. They had prospects. All their meals and uniforms were provided and they either had their own room in the attic or one of the eight servants' quarters snaking from the west side of the house. Other domestic staff would be found from outside in the village, such as a daily girl or charwoman and a laundry-maid. Plenty of gardeners and garden labourers lived close by as well as a bountiful supply of men and boys to work about the stables.

When Mr Giltrow arrived, Colonel Murray had been dead for nine years. The house had been sold up and used by The Whitton Park Sporting Club until 1900 when it fell on hard times. Frederick Hooper, a jobbing gardener from Bristol, his wife Elizabeth and their two daughters, Daisy and Annie, inhabited three of its rooms in 1901.

Discussing the fate of Whitton Park in May 1900, Twickenham Council's continued view was that in a county so rich in historic monuments, the expense of their adequate maintenance from county funds would effectively limit their other responsibilities, and that as a matter of national importance, such expense might more fittingly be defrayed from national rather than local resources. Lead by Councillor James Wills, petitions from members of the public supported by Heston & Isleworth UDC, joined the Earl of Meath as Chair of the Metropolitan Public Gardens Association in urging Twickenham Council to seriously consider stopping the sale. A substantial contribution towards the cost of acquiring the Estate for public use led to a long and protracted debate, but it was the purchase of Marble Hill Park that left Twickenham Council and the London County Council unable to take on Whitton Park and so was completely lost by 1934.

With ALL

WHITTON PARK.

Good Wishes

Having secured the details of probably the last occupants in what remained of Archibald Campbell's once splendidly equipped Greenhouse, John Burridge Giltrow took his leave via the drive, which in today's terms wound its way to the tip of Wills Crescent and into Park Avenue, opposite Carrington Avenue. Arriving back at the junction of Whitton and Hounslow Roads from what is today Park Avenue, Mr Giltrow passed by the empty Lodge to turn south in the direction of Holly Bush Corner.

At this time there was no South Western pub on the corner of Whitton Road and Whitton Dene. The fine redbrick Tudorbethan house opposite was then 10 years away. The wall we see today marking the southern limit of its grounds also defined the boundary between the parishes of Heston & Isleworth and Whitton. Numbers 1-8 Whitton Park Terrace (now 128 – 114 Hounslow Road) further south had only just been built when Mr Giltrow called by. In keeping with other limited development on the Whitton landscape at this time, these houses were built to attract respectable members of the lower middle classes.

Charles and Mabel Cooper occupied 1, Whitton Park Terrace (now 128). As a journalist and author, Charles Cooper would have witnessed across his 56 years the Victorians' thirst for print journalism that initiated the major structural developments forming the basis of our newsprint culture today. Newspapers became increasingly affordable after stamp duty on them was abolished in 1855, based on the idea that there should be no tax on knowledge. Technological developments included sophisticated printing machinery, the telegraph, which communicated news stories over longer distances, and the expansion of the railways, which revolutionised distribution.

The various Education Acts had created by the turn of the 20th century a mass literate and politically engaged audience across all classes. The first organisation of journalists was formed in England in 1883. Professional courses in journalism began to crop up in universities, and the concept of responsible, unbiased reporting became the standard of quality and professionalism far removed from the previous century's educated but poor sub-class inhabiting 'Grub Street' where they produced their gossip-ridden newssheets.

Even at the provincial level, aspiring Hampton born journalist Charles Cooper had access to a huge range of newspapers, including The Mid-Surrey Times and General Observer, The Chiswick Times, The Richmond and Twickenham Times, The Richmond, Twickenham and Barnes Herald, The Middlesex Telegraph and County Advertiser and The County of Middlesex Chronicle. Some were more successful than others. The Teddington and Hampton Times and Riverside Reporter, for example, was established in 1900 and closed that same year.

Number two, Whitton Park Terrace was yet to find a tenant, while at number three, celebrating in the name 'Fairview,' lived company secretary, Stanley Kershaw, his wife Victoria and their one-year-old son, Reginald. Number four was also unoccupied, with number five in the occupancy of carpenter, William Newson and his wife Louisa. Twenty-year-old William was following his father's occupation, while the younger son, Esme, impinged on the tone of the new development by working as a general labourer. Three younger children aged from 14 to 9 years completed the household.

Mother and son gardeners, Susannah and Frederick Galloway were living at number six, and at number seven was 61-year-old Thomas Head, manager of whatever business or occupation Mr Giltrow's variable penmanship makes indecipherable. Mr Head's 37-year-old niece, Margaret Knox, was listed as housekeeper. Calling on number eight and the end of Whitton Park Terrace, our intrepid enumerator's day turned decidedly sour when the occupant, declaring only himself to be 'Watts' refused to make any further declaration, going to abuse Mr Giltrow "in a most abominable manner using the most filthy language and threatening behaviour" if disturbed again.

Deciding to let the matter rest there, Mr Giltrow continued south towards the church and thereafter the relatively urbanized stretch of Whitton. Developed after the 1800 Enclosure Awards when the Hounslow Road became the more direct route between Hounslow and Hampton, before then travellers turned southwest at the village off Kneller Road (the King's Highway) for what is today Percy Road.

Seen in the distance immediately right of the church grounds was in Mr Giltrow's day numbers 1 and 2 Woodside House. Replaced today with numbers 90-94 Hounslow Road, this site represents the cornerstone of Louis Kyezor's missionary zeal, akin to the schemes of Sir Titus Salt and later George Cadbury, whose aims were to provide a healthy and architecturally satisfying environment based on industry. Kyezor's choice of location was indicative of his particular take on Victorian philanthropy.

Whitton's regeneration and Louis Kyezor's part in it can be traced to a letter in The Times dated 16 October 1869 from the Reverend W G Hawtayne, the first vicar of St Philip and St James. In it he states that it was Louis Kyezor who persuaded Morris Emmanuel to purchase Kneller Hall in 1845. This in turn led to a general resurgence on the east side of the village, including the establishment of the Royal Military School of Music and later a school for Whitton. When Charles Edward Murray appeared on the scene in 1850, he supported Kyezor in the creation of a separate parish and his many public-spirited endeavours.

When Kyezor first arrived in the district, however, the fabric of the village and its moral order was in a state of rapid decline. The few large country houses that existed were then at the end of their tenure and with them the ordering and provision of work.

Augustus Gostling held the Whitton Park Estate, with no interest in local affairs. As the area became less and less attractive to the wealthy, so too did the adverse effects on the poor. The 'Pigsty Rookery' where Kyezor chose to begin his enterprise was the most deprived area, comprising a nest of five dilapidated cottages set into half an acre of land occupied by 'the most desperate characters.'

The new arrival was warned to 'get out of the village as soon as convenient, or he might probably have his throat cut.' But Kyezor decided not only to stay but also to build himself a house in this lawless area, calling upon Scotland Yard for protection while his fortress was secured. Gotha House, as Woodside House was originally known, comprised a pair of semi-detached villas built in about 1844 and where Kyezor lived at number two. A sales catalogue of 1872 describes a 'Most desirable freehold villa residence…containing 10 rooms, good garden, pleasant forecourt with iron palisades and trellis work to the front, with a side entrance and delightful view from the bay window, good hall entrance, the path continuing through a trellis work to a neat pleasure ground with Summer-House erected thereon…'

The same sales prospectus for what was known as Kyezor Place also offers an insight as to the economic estimation of the locale at that time. The Particulars of the Six Lots for sale begged prospective purchasers to observe the pleasant situation on the road leading from Hounslow to Hampton, a short distance from the church and minutes from the Twickenham and Hounslow railway station. The 'pretty little village' of Whitton was declared a desirable opportunity for parties with limited means or daily travellers to town.

After 1872, the name Woodside was adopted and continued to attract the more gentile tenant. In 1901, Mildred Houghton was one of a series of widows living there on her own means. Joining her were her sons, Henry, a market gardener born in Peckham, his brother Charles, a poultry raiser, and their 24-year-old sister, Emily. Completing the household was another of Mrs Houghton's daughters, Amy Donaldson and her two young sons, Bruce and Victor, both born in Waterford, Ireland.

At 1, Woodside House lived Joseph Harbon, a 48-year-old foreman carman, born in the village of Heath Row, now the world's busiest airport. Charlotte, his wife, was born in Whitton, as were the couple's eight children aged between 23 and one year old. The oldest, Margaret, was married and recorded under the name of Spackman. Joseph, the eldest of her two sons was born in Aldershot in 1899 and her second son, Jacob, in Whitton a year later. Mother in Law, Mary Ann Holden and boarder Richard Johnson, a general labourer, completed the household. Both houses survived until 1972 when they were demolished to make way for the less architecturally challenged dwellings we see today.

Kyezor's twin Gotha Houses (pictured bottom left) represented the northern end of his development started in 1844. At the southern end was another pair, Swiss Cottage and a Beer House that survives today as the Prince Albert public house (centre). The row of shops to the fore came about in 1906 and was the site of an orchard at the time of Mr Giltrow's enumeration.

Kyezor's passionate embrace of the Temperance Movement did not prevent him from omitting a Beer House as part of his plans.

Building a Beer House here made eminent business sense. Some 30,000 licenses had been issued in England and Wales since the Beer House Act was passed in 1830, which probably assuaged the businessman's sensibilities. Sayad Hassan, a Persian immigrant is credited with running The Prince Albert Beer Shop in 1855 and reappears after the census of 1861 when Thomas Cushing was the beer retailer. Frankfurt Cottage was built next, attaching Swiss Cottage, so that by 1845 between Gotha House and The Prince Albert Beer House, the five cottages originally comprising the notorious 'Pigsty Rookery,' plus an additional cottage, presented a disparate span newly venerated as Kyezor Place.

In 1848, three Matilda Cottages closed the southern gap from Frankfurt Cottage. The following year 1-4 Jessy Cottages filled the northern gap between Gotha House and Kyezor Terrace. The three shops that also survive were added in 1857 to complete the scene. After 1871 all these buildings became known as numbers 1-19 Park Place and now comprise what survive as 88 – 66 Hounslow Road and The Prince Albert.

Number one Park Place (now 88 Hounslow Road) had been occupied by market gardener George Hills since 1861, the year his wife Eliza had given birth to their eldest son, Charles. Living with them when Mr Giltrow called was their 21-year-old nephew, Sydney Higgs, the son of George Higgs, the prominent market gardener, who died in 1883 and whose business passed over to Frank Peacock. He was working as a planter along with his cousin Alfred who had joined his father as a market gardener.

Numbers two and three Park Place were in the joint occupation of roadman labourer, John Warner. He and his wife Emma occupied number two, while their sons, Charles, a 25-year old bricklayer, and Ernest, a garden labourer five years his younger, occupied number three. Living with them at this time was a 10-year-old boy who would go on to celebrate all but a year of his centenary in 1989. From the garden of this cottage he first witnessed the horse threatened with the internal combustion engine and then man taking to the air.

On his return from the trenches after 1918, Ted Coster would become the second caretaker of the recently established Murray Park, a place he would rule with a rod of iron for decades to come. With the job came a home at number 6 Colonial Villas (now 26 Colonial Avenue) where he would rear rabbits and a pig at the end of the garden.

He would show as much bravery in saving a small girl from drowning in the lake, as he would anger at the owner of Whitton Dean Farm for allowing his cows to roam the park. At close on 100 years, dressed in his linen jacket and Panama hat, Ted Coster would raise the Union flag each day in his garden and later embark on a precarious bike ride to The Albert for his daily pint.

Charwoman Eliza Parfitt and her boarder, James Evan, a farm labourer, enjoyed the luxury of two rooms apiece at 4, Park Place. A decade earlier, two of the rooms billeted military bandsman Arthur Harwood, his Maltese wife, Houee, their son Arthur and sister-in-law, Ruby.

Sixty-eight year old widow, Marion Cooper from Scotland occupied the other two rooms together with her unmarried daughter Ann and her three children aged six to three. All the cooking and hot water for both families was done by means of an open fire and a shared tap. The water closet at the rear of the garden might well have been for the convenience of more than these two households, representing exactly the poor quality housing associated with both the moral and the physical condition of the working classes that so exercised reformer Louis Kyezor. When he set about his improvements he was ahead of the game, but it would be many years after Mr Giltrow's enumeration before the local authority expressed the will to force more unscrupulous landlords towards state legislature and Kyezor's way of thinking.

Number five Park Place (80 Hounslow Road) marks the start of Kyezor's original swathe of development begun in 1844. Here in 1901, Whitton born agricultural labourer William Reeves was living with his wife, Ada and their five young children. Next door was coal manager Joseph Clark with his wife, Margaret, their three sons and a niece. Islington born James Minton at number seven was another enduring resident of Park Place, recorded in 1881 with his wife Emma and their two sons, James and Albert. A decade later, James was a gentlemen's gardener and Arthur had arrived. By 1901 only Albert was at home, taking on his father's occupation, that of house painter.

As befitting his higher social status, general carpenter Ambrose Shepherd enjoyed the comparatively spacious abode at eight Park Place with his wife Jane and their five children. Similarly, painter and decorator Frederick Carter had recently moved from Kensington to occupy the four rooms of number nine with his wife Mary and their three sons. At number 10, general labourer, George Reeves, his wife Ellen and their one-year-old son, George, also had four rooms to themselves. A decade earlier, Sarah Hope shared the same space with her family of nine, plus a lodger. While the extra income provided was doubtless vital to the household economy, his expectations in the form of his own room would have had a profound effect on the squalor and hardships faced by the family, especially 37-year-old Sarah.

Rising first to lay the fire for a cup of tea and a round of toast, her days in the fields during the summer months began at 6 am and finished 12 hours later. Market days meant a 5am start, often working through to eight or nine o'clock in the evening. At about 8am, it was back home to prepare breakfast for her husband and children, then returning to work until one o'clock when it was time to feed the family again. Preparing an evening meal, washing and general housework would be done at the end of a long day. If it rained, work continued until it became impossible to carry on, in which case Sarah would be sent home with no pay. Wet days meant busier mealtimes, having to change soaking clothes for those that had them to change into.

Springtime in Whitton presented fields awash with narcissus, daffodils and wallflowers waiting to be cut for piecework, which was paid out in bulk and shared among the workforce. This was considered much less onerous than standing in the sheds counting, arranging and tying bunches for a penny a dozen. But even that was preferable to pulling radishes, arranging and binding them at the dizzy rate of two pennies per dozen. Commanding six to eight pennies a bushel was pea picking, which meant heaving a weighty basket across the fields to the roadside for the carter to load up. Most winter mornings meant being wet above the ankles picking Brussel sprouts or cutting Savoy cabbages dripping with dew or covered in frost.

A century earlier, women principally from Shropshire, Wiltshire, Ireland and Wales earned three shillings and sixpence by carrying on their heads a forty-pound load the ten miles to Covent Garden Market. Women also undertook even heavier tasks alongside male gas works stokers who were redundant in summer and Buckinghamshire tree fellers who worked in the beech woods in the winter. With no shortage of field labour, especially female, when Sarah Hope was pregnant she would hide her condition until the last possible moment. Sarah's daughters would find more lucrative and less crippling employment in manufacturing and the retail industry. Steam powered lorries and farm equipment would gradually reduce dependency on the horse and the consequent ready supply of manure. If Sarah survived into her 60's she would witness the unceasing march of development out of London that ultimately ended Whitton's agrarian status.

Except for their frontages, the three shops have altered little since they were built in about 1857. James Pullen, bootmaker, moved to Whitton from Chelsea in 1878 with his wife Mary, their seven children and James's brother John, an unemployed Grocer. On the night of 31st March 1901, 28-year old Wallace was the only offspring recorded at home and was now a carpet salesman at a time when most homes could only afford painted or stained floorboards.

A semblance of comfort might be provided with a rush mat, a rag rug, or a central square of carpet. Otherwise fitted carpets were only available to the exceptionally well to do. The development of mass-produced, machine-made carpets is a relatively recent innovation. From the 18th century towards the 1930s inventors strove to meet the challenges of high labour costs and loom width restrictions, and by the time Wallace Pullen entered the world of carpets, the sewing together of 27-inch wide strips of Broadloom weave was still the only method of producing a cover for more of the floor in a repeatable design.

One of the other two shops, then numbers 12 and 13 Park Place, continued into the new century as a Grocer's under the administration of Arthur Knighton. By then Mrs Knighton had given over her occupation of grocer's assistant to daughter Emily. The ranks of her siblings had grown from Annie and James to include nine-year-old Hilda. Business had blossomed too, with Arthur Knighton employing the services of a domestic servant, Ellen May Salter, a 20-year-old locally born girl.

Numbers 14 - 16 Park Place, formerly Kyezor's Matilda Cottages built in 1849, were occupied in 1901 by agricultural labourer, William White, who lived at number 14 with his wife, Harriet. A decade earlier and the four rooms quartered student bandsman, Silas Liddle and his wife Emma, and 22 years earlier was home to a fractious 82-year-old called Thomas Haydon Green, whom, but for his fierce temper would have no special place in Whitton's history. For it was on the morning of 11 October 1869, following a particularly venomous altercation with Louis Kyezor, his landlord, that Green shot him point blank in the stomach with a pistol.

Panic stricken, the assailant fled back to his cottage, grabbed another pistol and killed himself in the outside water closet. Louis Kyezor died in agony hours later. The subsequent inquest revealed that the murderer's name was really George Edwards, one of the band of conspirators arrested in Cato Street, Marylebone, in 1820, before they set out to assassinate the King's ministers. While his co-conspirators were decapitated or deported, Edwards, was subsequently revealed to have been the principal informant in the case of the Cato Street Conspiracy. He was given a new identity and found work at Somerset House until he was retired to the suitably obscure location of Whitton.

The murder made headline news and was reported in The Times in great detail the following day, condemning the actions of the "miserable madman of 82" specifically and "The Whitton tragedy" generally as but one of a "pile of horrors comprised in little more than a fortnight" plaguing the nation. Three days after his murder, Kyezor's body was taken from Whitton to Isleworth station to allow for the long procession to progress along Hounslow High Street.

Complete with a full complement of Rifle Volunteers, but no band, the blinds were drawn in houses along the route lined with many people who had gathered to pay their last respects. Later that day he was buried with full military honours at the Maiden Lane Synagogue cemetery off the Mile End Road in East London. Among the many tributes paid to him was that by members of the Twickenham Local Board in so far as "the parish of Whitton had lost a man to whom replace they would find great difficulty". The Times looked to Kyezor's advocacy of what he designated "Justice to the working people", a sentiment shared by the Vicar of Whitton, W G Hawtayne, who praised "the poor unlettered Jew" as "one of the best friends to Christianity in Whitton".

Number 15 Park Place was the second of Kyezor's three Matilda Cottages. In 1891 it was another billet made over for a married student of music at Kneller Hall. Unlike Arthur Harwood and his family occupying two rooms at number four, Albert Lavesock had the luxury of four rooms with his wife and two children. After him came wheelwright Thomas Jones who had moved to Whitton from Bristol in 1896 with his wife Mary. Their daughter Margaret was born in Whitton, as were her brothers, Albert and Alfred.

Living next to them at number 16 was George Cox, a coach painter and his wife Melissa, their 15-year-old son William, a railway signal lad, his younger brothers Bertie and Leonard. The youngest child was Gladys, aged one. Thirteen-year-old Bertie was a pageboy, a job description harping back to medieval times when small boys were employed as personal attendants. In 1901 Bertie might still have worked as part of a large household or more likely at one the grander or more stylish hotels in livery for door duty and to run errands.

Billeted in three rooms of the more spacious Frankfurt Cottage was Thomas Steele, another student at Kneller Hall, returned to England from duty in Bengal in 1891 with his wife and one year old son, also called Thomas. In the other four rooms lived Thomas and Mary Fry, who had moved to Whitton before 1872 when their daughter Rosa was born. Sons George and Arthur followed 11 and 17 years later.

By 1901, Thomas Fry had done well for himself. Now tenant of the entire house, he had changed his occupation to that of furniture remover. Mary no longer did other peoples' laundry and George declared his occupation to be that of horticulturalist.

Louis Kyezor probably chose the name Frankfurt Cottage out of his Germanic origins. Similarly the larger Swiss Cottage next door built in 1844 together with The Prince Albert Beerhouse. Listed as number 18, Park Place at the time of Mr Giltrow's enumeration, the lower half of Swiss Cottage was a Haberdashery shop with two domestic rooms occupied by widow Alice Philips. Living on her owns means in another two rooms was Sarah Drewett, also widowed. George Barton, a private in the Infantry was head of the household in the other three rooms with his wife, Jane.

George Barton may have seen duty in India or those parts of Africa that played out a familiar story of British colonialism throughout his military career. He would have been just old enough to take part in the Anglo-Zulu War fought in 1879, which signalled the end of the Zulus as an independent nation. The First Boer War was where the British army dressed in their bright red tunics proved no match for the bush fighters and was defeated.

With four sergeants, a quarter master sergeant and a drum major billeted either side of The Albert, such events would have served as major talking points among the regulars when Jesse Randall was the beer retailer. Or when the British government ordered Egypt to abandon the Sudan, or again the Second Boer War rooted in the discovery of the largest gold field in the world. Oliver Rodgers stood behind the bar of Prince Albert Public House when the failed coup d'etat sponsored by Cecil Rhodes culminated in the relief of Mafeking on 18 May 1900, provoking riotous celebrations throughout Britain. With the funeral in February 1901 of the nation's longest-serving sovereign now a memory, there was the coronation of the late Queen's popular and roguish son to look forward to by Thomas Perkins, beer retailer of The Prince Albert Inn, and Private Barton, now the only regular in uniform living on the Hounslow Road.

The sales prospectus for Kyezor Place in 1872 gives the particulars of Lot 1 as the 'old established freehold beer house, with bay window, good bar, sitting room, tap room, yard with side entrance, skittle alley, washhouse and four bedrooms'.

Also included were two shops and tenements adjoining and partly over the premises. Although extensively remodelled, what we see today is essentially the original combination of the Albert Beer House and Swiss Cottage built around 1844. The three Matilda Cottages (14-16 Park Place) were pulled down in the 1960s to create the Albert's car park. Frankfurt Cottage (formerly number 17) was also torn down in the 1960s and is now the site of The Albert's beer garden (to the left of this view).

Following Kyezor's murder, stewardship of all of his properties in Whitton was given over to his daughter, Matilda, who was appointed executor of his estate together with Colonel Murray. Within a year it became clear that Matilda's business acumen did not match that of her father. The properties were miss-managed and fell into decay.

By 1871 at least 12 houses formerly owned by Louis Kyezor were lying empty. Eventually a petition to salvage the situation was presented by one of Kyezor's sons. On 15 January 1872, all of the properties along Hounslow Road formerly known as Kyezor Place were sold. The Prince Albert is the only surviving property to retain its original name.

When John Burridge Giltrow stepped out of The Albert, all of the land opposite was a mass of ornamental and native trees representing a later addition to Whitton Park. Immediately south was the tail end of an orchard that reached down from the rear of Vicarage Cottage behind Kyezor's ribbon of development to the shops we see today. Now mostly altered to domestic use, The Parade arrived five years after Mr Giltrow's enumeration. Similarly the row of terraced houses south of them, concluding at the time with a high-class draper's shop, now The Imperial Café.

In 1901 the orchard ended at this point with an enclosure comprising four properties sold to Louis Kyezor in 1864 by a local resident, James Pearce. The cul de sac running beside the Imperial Café was at that time an access way known as Pearce's Road and which today boasts a flavour of Whitton's rural past in the form of a cluster of dwellings formerly known as Murray's cottages.

William Bradley had occupied the four rooms of 1, Murray Cottages since before 1891. When Mr Giltrow took his particulars, the 71 year old was suffering a growth on his intestines and was declared a pauper. His 66-six year old wife Harriet continued to work. Previously she had been a laundress, but Mr Giltrow's handwriting defies confirmation as to what provided the family income in the new century. With his wife Rachel and their five children, house painter Richard Windibank had taken over the tenancy of 2, Murray Cottage from James Hull, a night watchman at the Gunpowder Mills, Whitton's only manufacturing industry.

With its history of catastrophic explosions, the question of more suitable accommodation for its night watchman would not have been so much a matter of social reform as one of basic health and safety. For as well as the noise of small children throughout the day, there was the hustle bustle of the neighbouring cattle yard to contend with.

Although much altered, these rare survivors with their whitewashed walls and red-pantiled roofs all-too easily romanticise the quintessential rural idyll. Probably the larger cottage to the right of photograph opposite had changed its name to Albert Cottage by 1901 when it was occupied by Arthur Dean, a 39 year old domestic gardener, his wife, Annie, and their three children. Next to it, the quirkily shaped Albert Villa (below) also survives together with its generous yard (26a Hounslow Road). Until recently it was the base for a local scaffolding firm, which gave way briefly to an American style car wash.

The living and office accommodation adjoining the yard was in 1891 home to cattle dealer Richard Hunt, his wife, Maria and their son, Bertie. The business appears to have impacted badly on renting the more superior Whitton Villas fronting Hounslow Road at this point, with the noise and smell of cattle trading literally feet away from their tiny back yards. This was not conducive to the aspirant middle-class servant–keeping tenants for whom these villas were intended.

James Pearce was living in 1, Whitton Villas (below) in 1881 when he was aged 86 and retired. Then his son William was the head of the household and running the family Market garden business. William was born in 1842 in Whitton, as was his wife Louisa two years his junior. Their four children, William, Louisa, Robert and Welcom were aged from 18 years to seven months and all born in Whitton. By the time of 1891 census, the family had moved on and both Whitton Villas were unoccupied, probably due to the more acceptable backdrop of a market garden having given way to a cattle auction yard.

At the time of Mr Giltrow's enumeration Richard Hunt had also moved on and the yard appears vacant. Commercial clerk William Payne was living in one part of Albert Villa with his wife Emma. Number one Whitton Villas remained empty and in number two, Mr Giltrow found 70 year old Jane Pooley, living on her own means with her 69 year old sister, Mary and 64-year-old first cousin, Eliza Vicary, both of independent means. Catering for the needs of these three elderly ladies was general domestic, Sarah Truce.

Contemporaneous in style with Louis Kyezor's Gotha House, numbers 1 and 2 Whitton Villas (now 26 and 24, Hounslow Road) capture in their layout and appearance a flavour of the early Victorian architectural copybook ideal with Romanesque porches, bay windows and decorative bargeboards. Past precepts are utilised as sources for the few decorative embellishment of the exterior to offer the modest individuality of a mansion. Neighbouring Stanhope Terrace (now 22–12 Hounslow Road) survive as more modest, but none the less distinctive examples of villas indicative of late Victorian middle-class aspirational housing. The decorative embellishments of brickwork interlaid with bands of contrasting colour demonstrate where Victorian developers sought to include stylish features that would appeal to the taste of the upmarket tenant and maintain their occupancy.

The mix of occupations evident along this stretch of Hounslow Road in 1881, from labourers to servant-keeping households, indicates that the terrace was either partially completed at this time or was failing to attract the right sort of tenant. Certainly after 1891 it had established its credibility.

At the time of Mr Giltrow's enumeration, Life Insurance Agent, William Elden had recently moved from Enfield into 1, Stanhope Terrace with his wife, Martha and their three children. Somerset born William Escott was living on his own means with his Islington born wife, Charlotte, at number two. Frances Liddendale continued her occupancy of number three with her domestic servant, Emily Lewis, and next to them was spinster Ellen Cooper from Hyde Park living on her own means also with a domestic servant, 16-year-old Whitton born Alice Auderon. Number 5 was unoccupied. At the end of the Terrace lived Benjamin Franey a retired licensed victualler and his Whitton born wife, Emma. Next on Mr Giltrow's schedule were the architecturally less flamboyant numbers 1-4 Nevils Cottages, built before 1863 and demolished in the 1990s to make way for the small housing development now occupying the site.

Close inspection of the 1863 Ordnance Survey map shows a small drive off the road dividing the first cottage from the other three. This photograph taken prior to demolition confirms that number one (at the far end) was originally detached from the others and the space later filled.

This view in 1935 shows the business premises of local decorators and suppliers, Richards and Oliver. Sometime before the 1970s, the frontage was restored. Together with the other three units, it continued to house various businesses until the whole block was demolished.

In 1901, Norfolk born corrector of the press, James Mitchell and his wife Barbara were living in number one next to the premises of carpenter and joiner, Edward Grumett. In the previous census, these same cottages were scheduled as five and four Holly Bush Corner. Number Five was unoccupied and number four was a diary run by Whitton born widow Emma Sainsbury, assisted by her three sons, Alfred, Thomas and Walter, each in their 20s and recorded under their father's name of Nevells. Emma was widowed between 1861 and 1871 when her husband Thomas, a castrator, died. Before 1881 she was a cow keeper living and working at the same location. Her eldest son Charles aged 23, was a cowman, his younger brother, George, was a carman. Alfred, then aged 19 was a butcher and his 16-year-old sister (with an unreadable name) a dairymaid. Thomas aged 13 and Walter aged 11 were both at school.

By the time of Mr Giltrow's enumeration, Alfred Nevells was working at 3, Holly Bush Corner on his own account as a pork butcher. He had married Alice from Bermondsey who had given birth to their first son, also called Alfred, two years previously in Feltham. Their second son, Sidney, was born in Whitton two months prior to Mr Giltrow's visit.

In 1891, Daniel Pemberton a 49-year-old widowed tracklayer occupied 3, Holly Bush Corner. Next to him was a Grocer's shop run since before 1881 by Whitton-born, spinsters Jane and Elizabeth Anderson. Also recorded was a sister, Harriet, who was a 'pupil teacher', and brothers Charles and George. Only George, the youngest, remained with his two older sisters in 1891, by which time he had finished his apprenticeship as a printer's compositor. Joining the household was niece, Flora Coleopy, who was born in Ceylon, but registered as British subject. In 1901, the family's General Store was in the hands of 55-year-old widow, Emily Holland who was entertaining visitor, 10-year-old Flora Chandler on Census Night.

At 1, Holly Bush Corner, hidden behind the huge holly Tree that gave the location its name, lived William Anderson. Also locally born, he was no obvious relation to his near neighbours. In 1881, aged 29, he was a Master Baker employing one man and married to Helen with a daughter, Maude, aged three. By 1891 she was joined by eight-year-old George, six-year-old Alice and Robert aged two.

Presumably Helen died, as we find William Anderson remarried by 1901 to 43-year-old Louisa. Robert, aged 12 in that year, was still living at home and joined by eight-year-old Thomas, which suggests that Helen Anderson died at childbirth. Mr Giltrow includes an adopted daughter, Barbara, who was born in Bradford seven years earlier, clearly Louisa's child from a previous union. Robert, or 'Old Rob Anderson', as he is still remembered, continued in business on this same spot into his 80s selling homemade ice-lollies and individual cigarettes to boys who spent hours playing on the pinball machine. Rob retried after the arrival of decimalisation in the early 1970s. The shop is now one half of Jolly's Indian Restaurant. A private business now makes up the rest of Holly Bush Corner.

NELSON ROAD (WEST) TO HANWORTH ROAD

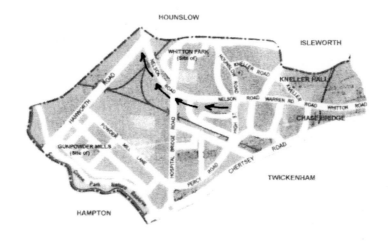

'....the Nelson Inn including Heathfield Farm & two cottages near the Railway Cottage near Hounslow Station.....'

Opposite Holly Bush Corner on the western side of Hounslow Road stood South Lodge, one of a number of former estate lodges marking the boundaries of Whitton Park. Although Mr Giltrow saw fit not to include it in his enumeration, South Lodge survived until the late 1960s when a hall in its grounds was used as The Vicky Burke School of Dancing. Today the site is occupied by a small set of apartment blocks. John Parker was recorded as the last Lodge keeper in 1871. A decade later coachman William Elsley was in occupation and in 1891 the Lodge was given over as a billet to Sergeant Major John Lancett attached to the Royal Military School of Music at Kneller Hall, his wife Elizabeth, her 75 year old mother, a widowed Aunt and son, 22-year-old son, George.

George Lancett was the fourth worker involved in the prevalence for print along the Hounslow Road. Journalist Charles Cooper was at one end of industry with corrector of the press James Mitchell at the other. In the middle were printer's compositors such as George Anderson and George Lancett. Their job was to set the typeface by hand using individual metal blocks with raised letters. A time-consuming task, not only was the typeface tiny but required great dexterity with the raised letters reversed to allow for the mechanics of printing. After the text, images, and various types of spacers needed to complete the page were locked into place, the likes of James Mitchell checked for errors.

Crossing to the south side of Nelson Road, John Burridge Giltrow ventured next into the fourth of Whitton's public houses, The Admiral (or Lord) Nelson, which opened as a Beer House before 1840, or around 35 years or so after the new highway later named Nelson Road had come about. One suggestion as to how The Nelson acquired its name is the circuitous connection with the Suckling family, whose estate at Whitton was close by. Sir John Suckling was the Stuart poet who is said to have invented the game of cribbage at Whitton. His father's half-brother's great grandson was Dr Maurice Suckling who had a daughter, Catherine, who was Horatio Nelson's mother.

The most likely naming of the beer house, however, probably coincided with the government plan between 1838 and 1845 to commemorate both the importance of the battle of Trafalgar and the immense popularity of its victor, which culminated in the Admiral's famous column and Trafalgar Square as the place to embrace it.

When in 1861 the landlord of the Admiral Nelson Beerhouse put in an application for a full licence, Louis Kyezor opposed it having previously discovered the applicant, Peter Neville, lying in the road in a drunken stupor partly undressed. Fortunately for the landlord, a local constable testified that Mr Neville was of good character, he had never seen him drunk and maintained that the house was always well conducted. A recently unearthed cartoon (overleaf) drawn by a local wag at the turn of the last century quite possibly depicts a degree of mutual benevolence that existed between the various landlords and the local police that persisted for many years.

The Nevill (or Neville) line was broken in 1881 when William Bicknell was the licensee, but resumed again in 1891 to 1901 when George Nevells (sic) was the Licensed Victualler, which dates the cartoon to that period. One of the Police Notices stuck to the wall of the pub is being disfigured with the word 'ROT', as soldiers from Kneller Hall advertising spurious services mingle with the crowds, mostly comprising children of all classes plying themselves or others with drink. The back of one sandwich board carried by a constable proclaims: 'Police Regulations Notice: Landlords are to supply the police with stimulants FREE OF CHARGE during the winter'. Another board declares that the Police will confiscate all Liquors found on children under 14.

The variable spelling of Nevill, Nevell, Nevells and Nevills permeating this corner of Whitton includes the sons and daughters of Emma Sainsbury, the dairy keeper at Holly Bush Corner. Emma was married to Thomas Nevell in 1870 but was widowed before 1881. According to the subsequent censuses she never remarried, the assumption being she assumed her maiden name.

George Nevell, the landlord of the Admiral Nelson, was Emma's eldest son. He was married but his wife doesn't appear in the 1891 census, only a seven-year-old son, also called George. Ten years later and May Nevell appears on Mr Giltrow's Schedule as George's wife, with a six-year-old daughter, Daisy, dating the new union to 1895. His son, also called George, who would have been 17 in 1901, does not appear in Mr Giltrow's enumeration.

Before The Admiral Nelson was 'improved' in the 1930s to that we see today, two mean cottages nestled at its western end fronting Nelson Road. Before 1891 they constituted the second pair of Nevell Cottages in the immediate area. Fifty-five year old Ann Roseam occupied one in 1881. As a monthly nurse she may have cared for women during their monthly cycle or as a confinement nurse, attending women during the first month after childbirth. Overall the definition of nurse at this time varies wildly. Ann's daughter Eliza was working as a photographer's assistant at a time when the new dry-plate photographic process created a market for the mass production of photographic portraits. The first studio to arrive in Whitton was in 1908 in the old chemist shop (now The Triangle Café) where the glazed roof section built to capture the northern light, still survives.

Next on Mr Giltrow's schedule were Nelson Cottages. A fragment of one of them is just visible to the extreme left of this view looking west along Nelson Road in about 1910. South Lodge and its grounds are hidden behind the fencing on the north side of the road.

In 1891 another widow, 86-year old widow Mary Clarke, shared three rooms of Nelson Cottages with her widowed grandson, Alfred Pearce, a general labourer. Despite advancing years, Mary still worked as a laundress. With none of the more prosperous households in Whitton employing a maid specifically to deal with the household washing, Mary Clarke would either go to the house to do the washing, or more often than not take it away to her own home. Taking in other peoples' laundry was an invaluable way to augment a meagre family income for a married woman. For a single or widowed woman it could be crucial.

The work was quite skilled and laundresses could make a reasonably comfortable living, but it was hard work over perhaps six days a week, often for the whole of their lives. Washing day for the ordinary working mother was a major event and due to the labour involved, it was also as infrequent as practicable. The less frequent the washing, the more affluent a family could show itself to be, with sufficient clothing to wear until next wash day.

A larger house might have its own laundry room and a more modest one a scullery, whereas the likes of Mary Clarke only had only a tiny back yard for washing in a copper tub using a pole called a 'dolly' or a small three-legged stool to plunge and agitate the clothes in the boiling water. Washboards were also used, which were quicker and easier to use. Stains would be rubbed hard with a bar of soap. Sometimes bleaches and a substance called 'blue' were used for white clothes, and starch for linens, aprons and collars, often regarded as a specialist skill of the professional laundress.

The whole process would have taken Mary most of the day, requiring an early start. When the items were fully washed and rinsed, they would be wrung out to remove excess water then hung to dry. If was wet, then they would be hung on lines inside the house on clotheshorses. Once nearly dry, and if there was access to one, clothes and bedding were put through a mangle to smooth them, sometimes taking the place of ironing, a process carried out using a series of flat irons of various weights and sizes that were heated on the stove or by the fire. Mary Clarke and her grandson were fortunate in comparison to many of their contemporaries in each having a room to themselves. But their conditions were no less onerous, sharing as they did the same back yard as The Nelson where the men's urinal vied for space with four families sharing one tap and a single outside closet.

Mary's days of endless washing were over by 1901 when her rooms were given over to 71-year-old Anne Fitzwater, who was 'kept on by her own family'. Next door lived Edward Hughes, a contractor's carman, his wife Charlotte and their four children variously born over the past nine years in Richmond, Ripley, Streatham and Twickenham. Both these cottages were demolished when The Admiral Nelson was rebuilt and enlarged in the 1930s,

Number one Westeria Place was where Arthur Rose had been running the Butcher's shop since before 1884, the year his wife Isabella gave birth to the second of their four sons, Ebenezer. Despite the modest size of his establishment, room was found for domestic servant, 15-year-old Alice Downes. Next door was the grocer's shop, run by Sarah Hathway and her son, William.

The shells of these two shops survive as a pair of blank, pebble-dashed domestic dwellings numbering 129 and 130 Nelson Road. The only physical clue as to their previous incarnation is the raised facade giving the impression of more substantial business premises.

Alma Cottages next to them were before 1901 occupied by a small contingent of police constables, possibly some of those depicted in the cartoon lampooning the goings on at The Admiral Nelson. From the regulation minimum requirements we know that all of these men would have not been below the height of 5ft 9ins, were able to read well, write legibly and have a fair knowledge of spelling and have 'a degree of intelligence'.

'Bodily dysfunctions' that would have prevented them joining the Metropolitan Police included flat foot, stiffness of joints, narrow chest and deformities of the face. A First Class Constable could expect to earn £80 per year, which included allowances to cover uniform and lodgings.

Recalling the famous battle of the Crimea War fought in 1854, Alma Cottages also survive. Man of means, Joseph Messenger occupied number one in 1901 with his wife, Fanny, a retired tailoress. In the four rooms of number two lived district council roadman, Thomas Hamilton, his wife Mary and their five children, and next to them was paperhanger Frederick Dunn and his wife, Ellen.

Hope Cottages recorded next by Mr Giltrow stood where the road now leads to Whitton library and the town park. Number two was occupied by 54 four year old Edmund Clark from Jersey, a general dealer working on his own account, his wife, Hannah, and their four children. Sarah Clark, the 96-year-old widow living next door at number three was no obvious relation. Her 60-year-old widowed daughter, Emma Watson is scheduled with her, as is lodger Alfred Pearce, who 10 years earlier was living with his grandmother a few doors down at number one Nevells Cottages. Together with the demolition of Hope Cottages went a clutch of glasshouses and part of a 2.7-acre market garden, probably worked by 65-year-old nurseryman James Pollington.

James and Sarah Pollington were living in Rose Cottage in 1901, having previously been sharing number three Park Terrace next door with Henry Collins, a gentlemen's gardener and his family. Living there in 1901 was Salop born tailor, David Williams, his wife, Mary, their daughters Sarah, a dressmaker working on her own account who was born in Canada, and Annie Glass, Sarah's younger sister by a year with her three-year-old son called James. Number two Park Terrace was unoccupied.

Ten years earlier it served as another billet for student bandsmen at Kneller Hall. Frederick Harris, his wife, May and their one-year-old son, also called Frederick, then occupied two of its rooms. Sergeant Richard Owen, his wife, Kate and two year old Stanley enjoyed the luxury of three rooms, while Band Sergeant Edmond O'Neill, his wife Elizabeth and their one-year-old son, William, occupied the whole of number one.

Fortunately for the landlords of Whitton, the building of the Married Quarters at Kneller Hall had no depressing effect on the market. In 1901, Alfred Brown, a traveller in the wine trade and an army pensioner was enjoying the whole of number two Park Terrace with his wife, Elizabeth and their four children. Whereas Park Terrace joined the ranks of Hope Cottages to make way for Whitton Library, Woodside Villas (now 161-169 Nelson Road) survive. Built around 1859, they once formed part of the Louis Kyezor property portfolio and bore his name until they were sold along with the rest of his estate in 1872.

Typical of Matilda Kyezor's disastrous stewardship, in an act of sheer vandalism she tore out the fireplaces, floorboards and doors until a court order was placed halting her activities. As Gotha House was renamed Woodside House after its sale, so were 1–4 Kyezor Villas removed of their reference to the philanthropic businessman who had restored the fortunes of Whitton and renamed Woodside Villas. Occupying number one in 1901 was market gardener Joseph Franklyn, his wife, Elizabeth and daughter, Ella, who had been born in Whitton 14 years earlier. Stone Carver George Philpott had been settled in number three with his wife, Annie and their six children for a year.

Philip Tewkesbury, a 38-year-old railway signalman from Dorset lived with his wife, Frances in 2, Woodside Villas and next to them domestic gardener, Thomas Hillier. Part of the market garden land to the rear has given way to the atypical 1960s Kneller Telephone Exchange and to some later housing.

Next John Burridge Giltrow called on the occupants of Alma Villas, which stood just before St Edmund's Roman Catholic Infants School. Dairy farmer, William Clifford was living with his wife, Helena, at number one. In the previous census William, who was then 16 years old, was living on the family farm further west along Nelson Road. In number two was Henry Chapman who was living on his own means with his wife, May. Kingsbury Cottage prior to Mr Giltrow's enumeration was split between William Murphy, a general labourer from Cork and his wife, Norah, who occupied two rooms. By 1901 the Murphys were gone, leaving Market gardener, Charles Biggens, his wife, Charlotte, and their four children to occupy the whole of the house.

It would be in 1935 that the Fathers of St. Edmund of Canterbury would start a mission at Kingsbury Cottage, building on part of the land the small, yellow-brick church we see today. The first regular provision for Roman Catholics in Twickenham was in 1893, just over 40 years since the Catholic hierarchy in England was restored since the Reformation. In the 17th century there was only a handful of inhabitants of Twickenham reputed to be papists. One was a fruiterer and the other, Lord Belasyse and his household in Whitton. By 1938, the development included St. Edmunds R.C. Infant School and twenty years later the new church of St Edmunds of Canterbury.

West of what is today St Edmund's Lane was The Retreat. As the name suggests this was a grander affair than any of the other dwellings visited thus far by John Burridge Giltrow. Studies of 20th century urban expansion cite distancing themselves between crime, poverty and disease as being central to late Victorian middle class aspirations, as though it was something new. Across any society in any age, escaping less salubrious locations is not intrinsic to what historians like to refer to as the 'suburban ideal'.

Retired contractor James Neal had lived in The Retreat with his wife, Mary Ann, since before 1891 and was sufficiently wealthy to maintain a domestic staff of three. Neighbouring Heath Cottage was in the occupation of John Strokham who was living on his own means with his wife, Harriet, having taken over the tenancy from Police Constable George Hamilton and his family of three, plus a lodger. Heath Cottage, Heath Villa and May Tree Cottage appear variously as each other on the 1891 census and that comprising Mr Giltrow's enumeration.

Florist James Richie who moved from Tooting with his wife, Marion and their eight children in 1895, occupied May Tree Cottage. Adding to an already complicated built landscape was number two Heath Cottage where Maurice Balls, a 29-year-old life assurance agent from Bradford had lived with his wife, Emily and their two small daughters since 1899. And finally there was Rose Cottage, the last of what estate agents like to call 'bijou' residences along this section of Nelson Road. Here lived James Maystrom, a 39-year-old stone carver who was born in Bristol. Jane, his wife, was born in York, their six-year-old son Digby in Lambeth, four-year-old Daisy in Kennington and one year old Thomas who was born in Wimbledon.

The Maystoms' itinerant lifestyle doubtless reflects the phenomenal growth of towns and cities in Britain in the late 19th century. The requirement for civic buildings, churches and housing created an unprecedented demand for artist-craftsmen such as he. Whereas large workshops of architectural and ornamental carvers flourished in many areas with the skills to tackle the florid styles of the day, James Maystrom, possibly in common with George Philpott also living along Nelson Road, may have found employment as monumental masons serving Twickenham or Hounslow cemeteries, both close by. Earlier headstones were carved for symbolic meaning rather than decoration, while throughout the Victorian era stone carvers offered a choice of intricate designs and extravagant embellishments indicating current fashion. The Retreat, Heath Cottage, Heath Villa, May Tree and Rose Cottage have all been replaced with a mixture of mid to late 20th century houses and bungalows, similarly The Cedars.

The Cedars was a large detached residence towards present day Constance Road and set back off the highway. Elizabeth Carr, a widow living on her own means had moved there from Camden Town with her three daughters and son Reginald, a 'club secretary,' before 1891. John Carter, a man of means from Notting Hill followed after 1891 with his wife, listed simply as 'J,' and their 33-year-old daughter, Eliza. Despite The Cedars' generous size, both households employed a single servant, doubtless relying on domestics living locally to augment their other arrangements.

The large white painted edifice at the junction of Nelson Road and Constance Road declares itself to be Trafalgar House. It appears for all the world to be one large, detached structure complete with its impressive flight of steps leading up to an original glazed screen entrance way set beneath a Romanesque arch. As well as its liberal coating of white paint, the building has undergone other alterations in its time. The spacious front drive survives, although now concreted over. The cast-iron railings enclosing the front garden were requisitioned during the Second World War in the mistaken belief that such metals would make tanks and shells.

In its heyday, one or more of Whitton's numerous gentlemen's gardeners would have clipped the privet introduced by the Victorians from Japan, which soon became popular as a hedging material. Laurel, rhododendron and other examples of ubiquitous Victorian planting would have punctuated a gravelled drive, complete with tiled path repeating its design as flooring in the large entrance hall. In more recent years, half of the rear garden has given way to housing comprising the aptly named Camellia Close. The impressive doorway appears to be original, suggesting a single residence.

Of the few houses named in the 1881 census, Fairlight, as it was then recorded, is one of them. Captain John Clarke of the Royal Fusiliers was living here at the time with his wife and their two children. A nurse, a housemaid and a cook complemented the household. Given this first record of occupation, it would appear that the exterior we see today is largely in its original state as the grandest single dwelling in Whitton. It adopted the name of Nelson's most famous battle after Mr Giltrow's enumeration, by which time the house was split as numbers 1 and 2, Fairlight.

Heading the household in number one in 1891 was 69-year-old Bermondsey born Richard Cole, who was living on his own means with his wife, Elizabeth, his daughter, also called Elizabeth, his son, Charles, a bank clerk like his cousin Herbert who was living with them. House estate agent, Robert Cullerne and his wife and son occupied number two, with call on a groom and a domestic servant. The Cullerne's had moved on before 1901, leaving the dwelling empty and number one occupied by man of means, Sydney Keith, his wife, Margaret and their two children. Twenty-year-old Clara Carol from Hoxton nursed both the children who were born in Whitton, and 23-year-old Emily Woolroph provided the general domestic service.

The Ordnance Survey map of 1894-96 shows two separate households. Revisions after 1910-11 shows the building as a single structure. Less confused and thoroughly embracing the precepts followed by the newly wealthy of orderliness and distinctive taste are later arrivals next door, set in this healthier part of the district enjoying distance from work and social inferiors.

Mercifully free of white paint and with their exteriors and heavily planted drive much intact are numbers 263 and 265 Nelson Road, formerly 1 and 2, Rosedale. Like Fairlight built 30 to 40 years earlier, these of the 1880s sought to attract the same desired class of tenant subscribing wholly to the principles laid down in the manuals of Victorian etiquette and household advice.

Such houses were designed to impress. The architectural and decorative style represents a strong reaction to the symmetry and balance of the Georgian era. Founded on a desire to reflect the construction on the outside, the lavish decoration and ornamentation intrinsic to the style is inspired by the architecture of castles and churches further enriched with better quality and more elaborate bricks, shaped roof tiles, stained glass, coloured floor and wall tiles, bay windows and elaborate porches and gables. By the middle years of the 19th century, the public rooms had moved to the ground floor, the bedrooms were on the first floor, with servants' bedrooms above them. However, before 1901 these houses were out of fashion and Art Nouveau was making rapid headway.

Number two Rosedale enjoys no entry in Mr Giltrow's schedule. Heading the household of number one was 39-year-old George Townsend, his wife, Jenny, their 15-year-old daughter, Gladys and general servant, Edith Burr. George Townsend was a surveyor working for The London County Council, a body that was created in 1888 to tackle the problems of slum clearance and new house building.

Born in Stepney, in what circumstances we don't know, George Townsend would have experienced first hand the nightmare existence suffered by the Capital's poorest. His job would have brought him into direct contact with scenes as evocative of his birthplace at the turn of the 20th century as they were when he was a small child. As a white-collar worker George Townsend was automatically regarded as superior to someone in trade, but inferior to others. The Victorian class system was so rigidly defined that it was not easy to shift position. That was defined by background. And a profession was only as good as an address. Whitton was then, as it remains, a modestly priced settlement for the aspirant lower middle classes.

The housing we see today between Rosedale (263 and 265 Nelson Road) and Evelyn Close was in Mr Giltrow's day the site of The Nurseries, run by Ben Matthews since around 1850. A widower before the 1891 census, the nurseryman and florist was still enjoying the company of his sons, Ben and Stanley, and his daughters Emily and Stella a decade later. Mary Rossiter, his sister in law, had been replaced as housekeeper by Mary Hills who was assisted by domestic housemaid, Rebecca Shead. The Nurseries as a homestead was of a reasonable size, set in two and a half acres of land half filled with glasshouses. Eighteen-year-old Ben assisted his father as nurseryman while his sister, Emily, acted as bookkeeper.

Past what is today Evelyn Close, Mr Giltrow stopped next at Tithe Farm, which had been operated by William Clifford since before 1890 with the help of three labourers and a boy. Mostly grazing towards Powder Mill Lane and Hanworth Road, 12 of the 105 acres included all the land between Nelson Road, Hospital Bridge Road and The Whitton Railway Curve, otherwise known as The Feltham Curve or again, The Hounslow Loop.

Laid in 1847 when the London and South Western Railway Company secured the route from the then terminus at Richmond to Datchet (now the Windsor & Eton service), the loop provided for a service from Waterloo to include Barnes, Kew, Isleworth and Whitton Park. Twickenham station opened in the 1840s, but Whitton would have to wait another 90 years for one of its own. Twelve acres of the former farmland are now covered with predominantly inter-war housing, except for a high-density housing estate built in more modern times within the triangle of land enclosed on all sides by railway tracks.

Dotted about this immediate area in 1891 were a couple of Railway Cottages situated towards the northern exit of what is today Collingwood Close. One was occupied by Signalmen S.W.R Henry Cailes and his two sons, and the other by William Pink, his wife, retired father-in-law and a niece. Benns Cottage was, a tiny two-roomed affair on the south edge of Whitton Park, probably a former estate Lodge. Numbers 1 and 2, Wells Cottages sat along Hospital Bridge Road, roughly at the mouth of present day Vincam Close.

As The War Department had catered for married student bandsmen attending Kneller Hall, so too by 1901 had the London & South West Region Railway improved the living conditions of its employees. A terrace of eight, neat, solidly built houses imaginatively dubbed Railway Cottages now stood regimented south of the railway bridge at the bend of what is today Rodney Road. Behind them, where (at the time of writing) a forlorn late 20th century local authority facility languishes boarded up, stood a pair of higher-status railway dwellings called South Western Cottages.

Mr Giltrow records number one Railway Cottages as unoccupied. In number two was railway signalman Tom Rainer, his wife, their two young daughters and boarder, Sydney Holloway, a fellow signalman. Next to them lived signalman George Scott and his wife, Mary. Occupying number four was Charles Barker, yet another signalman with his wife, Sarah and their son, Charles, who broke the mould as a railway porter. Alfred Humphries, a railway platelayer was living in number five with his wife, Martha and their two young sons.

Frederick Godfrey and George Stevens, fellow platelayers, occupied numbers six and seven respectively with their wives and children. Concluding the inhabitants of Railway Cottages was Daniel Pemberton and his family. Quite why signalman John Brown and his wife and son enjoyed the relative opulence of South West Cottages isn't clear. William Pink, however, by now the longest serving railway signalman working 'The Curve' was probably deserving of the upgrade in accommodation. But soon, however, this noisy, steamy corner of Whitton would become as unrecognisable as it would be a cautious place to live. Although hugely declined since the 18th century when smallpox was as large a killer as heart disease and cancer are today, the dread of the 'speckled monster' was still apparent in Mr Giltrow's day.

Smallpox struck rich and poor, killing labourers and aristocrats without mercy. Between 20% and 60% of those infected died. The survivors were scarred for life and many blinded. Following the Infectious Disease Prevention Act of 1880, a circular was received by the Twickenham Local Government Board regarding a somewhat impudent scheme jointly forwarded by Richmond and Heston & Isleworth Local Boards for an Isolation Hospital to be built 'in the confines of Twickenham Parish'. In strenuous opposition of such a scheme, they were forced to build a joint hospital at Mogden, which came about in 1885 on the site now predominantly occupied by Tesco.

When Twickenham's Medical Officer raised the question of dealing with cases of contagious diseases it was found that existing accommodation in the district was severely limited and exacerbated by the large increase in the overall population, estimated at 21,000. Attention turned to the seven acres of Charity Land opposite Tithe Farm, described as being 'quite removed from any residential properties and therefore most suitable'. The Reverend R G Robinson, vicar of St Philip and St James, together with a number of residents, including William Clifford whose dairy farm was only yards away disagreed vehemently with the proposal, but their objections were overruled. But as the land was being cropped of 'trees, rye grass and mangel wurzels', preparations were halted on receipt of a complaint from a developer about to erect several houses in the neighbourhood.

At stake, however, was the health of a rapidly increasing population occupying denser housing conditions and an authority totally unprepared for another outbreak of small pox. In Twickenham there had been no cases of the dreaded disease reported from 1893 to 1901, but the prevalence of small pox in London and districts immediately adjoining Whitton was a cause for concern. The figures had risen from zero in 1899 to 144 in 1901, the same figure recorded six years previously. Nine years later, after often-farcical negotiations, the dread of smallpox had all but passed. Concern turned to scarlet fever and diphtheria and so the hospital was built, but way below the agreed costs and in the absence of proper plans, leaving a deeply unimpressed District Auditor to believe that 'some unfortunate inferences might be drawn'. The facility survived until 1938 when the joint Isolation Hospital at Mogden was enlarged to create a new South Middlesex Isolation Hospital, to include Twickenham.

In this prospect of the Isolation Hospital (c1910) looking west on Nelson Road, Hospital Bridge Road bears to the left. The building in the foreground was that belonging to Tithe Farm. Nelson Road continues to the right towards Hanworth Road and the next leg of Mr Giltrow's enumeration.

HANWORTH ROAD TO THE GUNPOWER MILLS

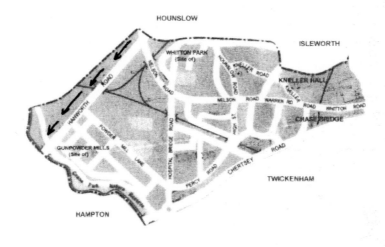

.....Mr & Mrs Clarke's House, The Lodge at Hounslow Cemetery, two cottages in the Hounslow Road, all the houses & Lodge at the Gunpowder Mills.....

Even lifelong residents are surprised to learn that Whitton's western boundary spreads as far as Hanworth Road, and then a good 500 yards beyond that to kiss the fringe of what today passes for Hounslow Heath. At the beginning of the 19th century, Hanworth Road was a country lane running parallel with Percy Road (part of which now forms the High Street). East and west of both these tracks was open heathland, punctuated predominantly by Whitton Park to the north and the Powder Mills to the south. Before the Enclosure Awards of 1800 and 1808, Whitton's western boundary included where we find today Wyndham Crescent at the junction of Wellington Road, all that adjoining the Hounslow Heath Nature Reserve towards Hounslow Cemetery and south as far as the River Crane.

In 1901, this section of Mr Giltrow's enumeration began at a farm variously given on maps as Heathfield or Heath Farm. Neighbouring Rosalind Villa is not marked. Outside of the census returns there is no other reference to it to be found in the Local Studies Collections of either Richmond–upon-Thames or Hounslow; a sure sign we have arrived in cross-border country where the parochial lights of local history tend to glow dim. By a process of deduction we can be reasonably sure that Rosalind Villa occupied the northern corner of Nelson Road at the junction with Hanworth Road, and that Heathfield Farm stood on the southern corner. Both were accessed via the same railway bridge we see today and that which Mr Giltrow crossed after calling on the occupants of South Western Cottages.

Logic dictates that both he and previous census enumerators would call first on the occupants of Rosalind Villa to the north and then south for Heath Farm en route towards the Powder Mills, but none did. With that conundrum in mind, Heath, or Heathfield Farm had ceased to be a farm since before 1891 when Charles Coles lived and worked there as a butcher with his wife Sarah and their eight children. The two eldest daughters, Lucy and Annie were dressmakers. The eldest boy, 14-year-old Charles, was following in his father's footsteps. Come 1901 the house was occupied by Charles Neale, a sergeant with the Twickenham Police, his wife Pheobe, their five young sons and one month old Ellie, who was born there. The house has subsequently been demolished and a block of flats now occupies the site.

Crossing to the north of Nelson Road to what is now Nelson Gardens, Rosalind Villa was enclosed in grounds dominated by glasshouses. It had been the home and business premises of Northampton born florist, William Clarke probably since 1869 when his wife Jane gave birth to their eldest daughter Eliza in Whitton. Their second daughter, Jane, was born two years later, and their brother Frank 13 years after that in 1883. Only he was at home on Census Night 1901, recorded as a florist like his father. By this time the gradual shift southeastwards of fruit and flower growing had seen Kent all but take the mantle 'Garden of England' from West Middlesex. Already large areas of Isleworth, Twickenham and Teddington had given way to housing. However, business remained good for William Clarke who could now afford a domestic servant in the form of 25-year-old niece, Bessie Brown from Isleworth.

Daughters Eliza, a dressmaker, and Jane, a milliner, had presumably moved on, suitably prepared for a world wherein a woman's position in society and her wealth could be immediately distinguished by her dress. For the refined 'lady' of this period it was essential to have clothes that were suitable for the occasion, which often meant a frequent change of dress. The hats Eliza would have made, often decorated with flowers and fruit, were an essential accessory worn by all women across all classes, indoors as well as out.

Eliza and Jane Clarke came from a family with enough money to pay for them to be apprenticed to learn their trades as part of an old, established system that promised a decent and respectable living. Middle and even upper class 'distressed gentlewomen' finding themselves put in the position of having to support themselves often turned to needlework. At a time when the growing middle classes were creating a new demand for low-cost, ready-made clothing, tailoring was shifting from the skilled male artisan to the cheaper option of women labour. Serving this growing market, many women worked at home for very low rates sewing ready-made clothing, known as 'slop-work'. Victorian London had been shocked with horror stories of young needlewomen, living and dying in miserable conditions, but the sweatshop thrived as a mainstay for predominantly women labour.

Whitton's boundary with Heston & Isleworth only just contained William Clarke's nursery and drew a distinct line between the urban development reaching out from the direction of Hounslow Town and unspoilt countryside. Hanworth Road was still a country lane. Today a small tract of open heathland survives in the form of a recreation ground set between Wyndham Crescent and Simpson Road. Nothing comprising the modern built landscape predates the First World War, except possibly for a humble structure tucked beside the rise of the railway bridge at the mouth of Conway Road.

In 1891 this was yet another Railway Cottage, occupied by S.W.R signalman Albert Browning who had recently moved to Whitton from Egham in Surrey with his wife, Annie and daughter, Alfreda. Presumably Albert Browning or his successor was enjoying improved living accommodation elsewhere, as Mr Giltrow fails to list the cottage in his enumeration. The building we see today is the same long, thin construction that appears on maps of the period, but is much made over with new windows, pebble dashed and painted exterior walls. Only a few original ridge tiles remain.

Mr Giltrow would have experienced no problem pausing on the brow of the railway bridge to enjoy the view. Today, the pedestrian is confined to a narrow passage on the west side. John Burridge Giltrow could amble about as he pleased, gazing east across acres of fields and trees interlaced with quiet country lanes as far as Richmond Hill and Hampton Court. To the west, the sprawl of Hounslow Heath was thus far free of the massive concentration of steel rails that would within a decade comprise the Feltham Marshalling Yards. Before then and embraced by the solitary curve of railway track south of the bridge was Hounslow Cemetery, controlled by the Hounslow Head of Guardians, but contained within the borough of Twickenham. What we see today is little changed from that laid out in 1869 as a typical Victorian public cemetery.

The trend for landscaping public cemeteries translates to a degree at Hounslow, where elements of garden design play a part in the lay-out of paths and the planting of yew, cypress, and juniper trees. The severe twin Mortuary Chapels for Anglicans and Nonconformists survive, as does The Lodge where Mr Giltrow called next.

James Clement, a 40-year-old Whitton born man had been sexton for the past 18 years. Cardiff-born Elizabeth Clement had filled its minuscule space with seven children, and found room for boarder, George Cottle, a relation, who was a cycle mechanic by trade. In their occupations, the Clements' eldest children further capture the diversity of the times. Fifteen-year-old Arthur worked as a cattle boy, while his older sister, Lavinia was a draper's assistant at a time when the working conditions of many shop workers were primitive.

Wages were low and working hours were long. On the shop floor, hefty fines could be imposed for each customer leaving the premises 'unserved' or not having been introduced to at least two articles. Strenuous efforts had been made to form a trade union organisation for shop assistants and at under 18 years of age, Lavinia Clement was granted a 74-hour week by the Shop Hours Regulation Act of 1887, but which for lack of inspectors was never operated.

As the Labour Party was galvanising Trades Union representation, The National Union of Shop Assistants was founded, followed by the United Shop Assistants' Union. But many shop assistants considered themselves above joining a 'trade association', which matched the opposition unions faced from employers. For many years to come, therefore, the shop assistant was required to be 'eternally young, infernally civil; have the polish of a cabinet minister and dress like a duke on the wages of a dustman'.

Ten years after Mr Giltrow left Cemetery Lodge, a 200 ft. diameter circular enclosure to the rear of the burial ground would be recorded as Whitton's single ancient monument. Sadly it was even then 'all but perished' with 'the slightest depression in the ground only just discernible'. The site (pictured above opposite) is now enclosed off the access road to the new Post Office sorting depot in Godfrey Way. Designated a Class C example of British-Romano earthwork, it was a simple round enclosure, as the geology hereabouts does not lend itself to impressive defensive works. Contemporaneous with Cemetery Lodge and the Mortuary Chapels, Glebe Cottage (below opposite) at the junction of Godfrey Way and Hanworth Road is another rare survivor along this route.

In 1901, Glebe Cottage was home to Robert Locke, a greengrocer who was born in Richmond, Surrey. He married Ellen from Reading around 1890 and was living in Chelsea a year later when their son Robert was born. Five years later they had moved to Twickenham where their son, Albert, was born and then daughter Eva. Their closest neighbours other than the Clements at Cemetery Lodge was Frederick Coles, a 58-year-old cattle foreman from Northampton, his wife Jane, their 16-year-old farm labourer son, William, and daughter Alice. They occupied Andrews Farm, a smallholding hugging the parish boundary where the Mill Farm Business Park is situated today. Otherwise, this entire area south of the railway track was almost all open country and unoccupied, and for a very good reason. The Gunpowder Works on Hanworth Road was one of a series of mills set up on Hounslow Heath since medieval times, creating highly precarious regions in which to live.

Because of the lack of domestic saltpetre supplies most gunpowder was imported until the reign of Henry VIII. During the reign of Elizabeth I, England's increased naval prowess meant an end to its dependency on Europe for supplies of the key ingredient to the making of black powder. The status of the powder mills on Hounslow Heath was further enhanced in the reign of James I, who granted a Royal Charter to the manufacturers working there. The census of 1881 includes John Elliott, a Scottish born foreman saltpetre-maker and refiner who came to Twickenham before 1875, where and when his youngest son was born. His eldest son, John, was born in Demerara, one of the original British colonies joined to British Guiana, now Guyana. His eldest daughter was born in St Lucia and her two younger brothers, Edmund and Douglas in Lincolnshire and Durham respectively.

The mill on Hanworth Road (now the site of Crane Park Nature Reserve) was established after 1766 when it was converted from a corn mill to the manufacture of gunpowder. In 1772 it was one of three powder mills that blew up, shattering windows for miles, including those of Horace Walpole's house at Strawberry Hill. The first explosion attributable to Whitton's Mill, but known as the Hounslow Mill, was in April 1774 when a massive explosion terrified people at church in Isleworth. Between 1796 and 1812 a series of disasters killed 30 workers.

Another serious explosion in 1872 caused one Hounslow resident to complain to the *Middlesex Chronicle* that the offending works was in the parish of Twickenham and not in Hounslow, thus offering a false impression that the latter was an unsafe place to live. The last major explosion was in 1887. In his science fiction fantasy, *War of The Worlds*, H G Wells wrote of violent explosions leading to speculation of violent volcanoes erupting west of London. 'Were the powder mills at Hounslow ready as a snare?' the citizens wondered as the Martians closed in on the capital.

In 1820, the firm of Curtis and Harvey acquired the Mills and ran them for the next hundred years. Under their management, the safety record improved but there were still many accidents until strict safety rules were introduced forbidding smoking and the carrying of any form of lighting or metal object that might cause a spark. Special clothing included felt shoes and trousers without turnups that might accumulate stones or grit. All floors and platforms of buildings were to be kept wet. In the event of a thunderstorm, the buildings were closed up and all personnel cleared from the vicinity.

The industrial buildings were all placed at some distance from each other. Those that carried out the more dangerous processes of manufacture were made of the lightest materials and carefully secluded by the mounds of earth we see today. This meant that should an explosion occur, then the least resistance was offered in the resulting blast.

Regardless of these very real dangers, the managers and their domestic staff were housed in a large enclosed bastion collectively known as Hanworth Lodge situated on the west side of Hanworth Road (now Grafton Close) directly facing the works. It was formerly the home of Lady Laura Dalrymple, who presumably experienced first hand the occasional discharge from her volatile neighbour. All the more curious then that on her death in 1834 she stipulated that her mother, the Countess Dysart, should live in the Lodge for the remainder of her life.

When the Countess died in 1840, Hanworth Park, including Hanworth Lodge, was sold to a Mr Henry Perkins to increase his holdings in land locally to 463 acres. Between then and 1891, The Lodge was leased or acquired by Curtis and Harvey. It comprised the big house itself set behind two smaller buildings, possibly number two and three Powder Mill Cottages, as given on the 1891 census, where yard foreman, John Brown, his wife and son were accommodated, and John Francis, a farm servant, with his wife, Ann, respectively. The Works Manager, William Brown, continued to occupy Hanworth Lodge together with a Housemaid and a Cook as he had done since 1881 when his wife Lucy was alive.

A series of watchmen's lodges stood along Hanworth Road and what is today Powder Mill Lane to the north, which, according to the 1881 census were habitable. Powder Mill Lodge was probably one of the two larger buildings in the grounds, which was occupied since 1873 by John Knight, the Assistant Manager, his wife Emily, their three children and two domestic servants. Number two Powder Mill Lodge contained watchman, Francis Spiers, his wife Ann and their six children. In number four was William Spanswick, foreman box maker, his wife and their two children. Numbers five, six and seven, were unoccupied. In number eight lived domestic coachman, William Andrews.

Possibly one of the work's longest serving employees, William Andrews is recorded on site in 1881 with his wife, Fanny and two children, Alfred and Mary. Alfred was then aged 22, working as a cooper and recorded as being deaf and dumb. Sixty year old horse keeper, Henry Farmer, his wife Henrietta, also appearing on the 1881 census were now sharing number nine with their 27 year old widowed son Harry and their 4 year old Grandson, also called Harry.

Arthur Darnford was the Works Manager in 1901, living in Hanworth Lodge with his wife, Emily, with no domestic help. The previous muddle of Powder Mill Cottages and Powder Mills Lodge was laid out on Mr Giltrow's schedule as simply 'Gunpowder Mills' and where John Brown, now 62, was still the yard foreman. His wife is no longer listed, nor his son, only a daughter-in-law, Winifred. A new post of Gatekeeper appears in the schedule, held by Henry Bricknell, living at the mills with his wife, Annie and their three children.

Harry Farmer was still living with his grandfather, Henry, the horse keeper, who was now 70 and with a new wife, Mary Ann from Walton. Scheduled next was Sussex-born coachman John Balchin, who had arrived in Whitton three years earlier with his wife Elizabeth. Both of their sons, three-year-old John and one year old Charles were born in Whitton. Farm baliff was another new occupational listing and one held by George Boxall, who had arrived in Hounslow from Guilford where four-year old Florence was born. Mary Jane Boxall had given birth to twin boys, Charles and George in Hounslow in 1900.

Assistant Manager, John Knight, now aged 61, had clearly been overlooked for promotion. Despite the arrival of Arthur Darnford as Manager, John Knight declared himself to hold the same post and, unlike his superior, retain two domestic staff to help his wife manage the household. Next, Mr Giltrow lists railway carter, George Langley, his Whitton born wife, Minnie and their five children who had all been born in Hanworth from 1876. Concluding the staff resident at The Gunpowder Mills is Domestic Gardener, Henry Aussand, his wife, Eliza and their son, Henry.

In 1927 a private buyer purchased the works and then sold on much of the land to Ideal Homesteads Ltd., for housing development. A band of riverside was purchased by Twickenham Council, and is today the Crane Park Nature Reserve. Through landscaping and with all the buildings gone, the most prominent feature remaining is what is generally known as the Shot Tower, although it's a matter of conjecture as to what its true purpose was. Proponents of the watchtower theory claim that a furnace used to melt the lead to drop into a vat of water to produce the shot would have presented an unlikely risk. However, the numbers of coppiced willow trees spread throughout the reserve bear witness to large-scale charcoal burning with the same inherent dangers. Indeed, after almost a century, much of the soil is black from charred wood.

For a shot tower to work properly it needed to be at least 100 foot high, and the tower at Crane Park is only 80. Early illustrations of the works show the tower boasting a belfry at its height and later with a clock mounted on it. More likely then it was a watchtower. Later still the structure was used for a brief period as a pumping station, used to help keep up the head of water. As water drained from the reservoir driving the wheel, additional machinery in the base of the tower would pump it up to the weir-head again. Unfortunately this activity lowered the water level downstream to such an extent that it resulted in court action and so was halted.

The massive folds of earth mounds we see throughout Crane Park today were built to deflect explosions into the air. The restored millpond cascades water over remnant sluice gates, which are still used to control the depth of water by means of wooden boards. The curved underbelly in surviving brickwork indicates a large water wheel of the undershot variety, which attached a shaft powered by gears to provide power to the works. Granite grinding wheels either complete or in fragments are scattered about the site, as are the foundations of buildings buried in the rich ground flora and mixed deciduous woodland.

The wharf by the tower provided a harbour for shallow draft barges that may have once transported the lethal cargo to the Thames at Isleworth, although it seems this was carried out by horse and cart, between 300 and 600 barrels of powder a week. All in all, the powder mills was a place of much and varied activity, utilising all of the technical, mechanical engineering and artisan skills of its periods in time.

The workforce recorded by John Burridge Giltrow in 1901, however, reflects a meagre impact on Whitton's workforce. At its peak in 1860 there were 320 men, women and children working at the Powder Mills and over 100 throughout the First World War. Those finding their way into the district's census records were predominantly management, their support staff and key workers. Clearly then there was a history of the workforce drawn traditionally from the Hanworth, Feltham and Twickenham areas, offering yet another indication of Whitton's confused sense of place, further compounded by the Post Office at the turn of the last century. When a charge of sixpence was made for the delivery of a telegram addressed to Whitton School, Twickenham, it was shown that although Whitton was in the borough of Twickenham, it was in the postal area of Hounslow.

An application made to the Postmaster General for Whitton to be included in the Twickenham postal area was rejected on the grounds that Whitton was more associated with Hounslow and that any alteration would provoke more public complaint than it would assuage. Telegrams addressed 'Whitton, Twickenham' were apparently rare. In pursuance of the same matter in 1914, the Commandant of the Royal Military School of Music wrote to the GPO. In their reply to him, The Duke of Northumberland's river was erroneously cited as 'a natural and clearly defined boundary' between Hounslow and Twickenham and that 'any other would be an arbitrary one; confusing and inconvenient to persons on both sides of the boundary'.

Whitton Park as an address was cited as that used for houses either side of the former estate. Also, the closest railway station for Whitton was Whitton Park (now Hounslow), which would have also lead to confusion. As well as several houses in Whitton Dean Road probably having to remain in the Hounslow area, so too would the Gunpowder Mills on the Hanwell (sic) Road. In conclusion, the General Post Office believed that not even significant increases in the population of Whitton could justify such a change and would in all probability reverse the benefits of the existing service.

It was the outbreak of war in 1914 and the heightened need for effective telegram communication that resulted in the speedy resolution to this long-standing issue. Having full regard to previous objections, and on receipt of an assurance that such a change would be acceptable to all affected, the Postmaster General was prepared to carry out the alteration. All households were leafleted, explaining that from 15th October 1914, telegrams for Whitton would henceforth be delivered from Twickenham. However, since the Gunpowder Mills had bourn the address 'Hounslow Gunpowder Mills' for many years, it was felt that no advantage would be accrued by changing its name; similarly Hounslow cemetery and Lodge.

POWDER MILL LANE TO HOSPITAL BRIDGE ROAD

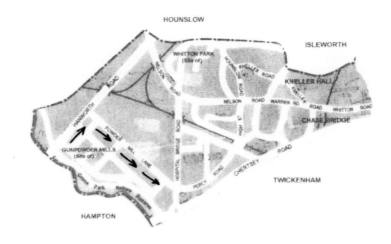

....The Lodge at Twickenham Cemetery, The Cottage occupied by Mr Lever....

The strict safety procedures in operation at the Powder Works meant that John Burridge Giltrow had no option but to backtrack along the Hanworth Road to Powder Mill Lane where he turned southeast for the penultimate leg of his journey. The Duke of York public house we see today on the corner of Hanworth Road and Powder Mill Lane was built in 1936 and named after an older drinking house in London Road, Twickenham, which was closed earlier that same decade when the proprietor transferred his business to the newly developing location.

In 1901, this and the whole area south of Powder Mill Lane was a green wooded barrier safely containing the hazardous works. On the northern side was arable fields and market garden land as far as the railway line. Today, where the shops and houses end along the northern side of Powder Mill Lane is another, more recent, cemetery administered by Hounslow Council on Richmond borough land. Complementing this rare, open aspect is the Heathfield Recreation Ground, which leads the eye towards Bridge Farm Nursery with its glasshouses, sheds and open land offering the sole surviving vestige of Whitton's agricultural and horticultural heritage.

The original Heathfield School along this stretch was built in 1931, since when its footprint has grown to include a plethora of 'temporary' huts, evidence of Whitton's rapidly increasing population thereafter. At the corner of Powder Mill Lane with Hospital Bridge Road there is to the left the somewhat 'Moderne', 'sun-trap' or 'International Style' Whitton Clinic, hovering somewhere towards the latter end of the Art Deco style. Devoid of much decoration and decorative objects, instead it typically stresses the use of function with its use of red brick and (until their replacement) galvanised iron window frames.

Neither this crumbling edifice nor the long-demolished Infectious Diseases Hospital half a mile north gives rise to the naming of Hospital Bridge Road. Although generally dismissed as historically insignificant, it is reasonable to mention this immediate area's connection with Knights Hospitallers who were granted a stretch of Hounslow Heath in 1300 and where they remained until the dissolution of their house in 1539. 'Whitnne' Bridge (now Hospital Bridge) was then a crossing of the River Crane towards Hampton.

The more widely accepted root of the hospital association, however, dates to 1685 when James II succeeded his brother Charles II. In the face of much opposition from the establishment and population at large due to his open Catholicism, he gathered an army here.

Hounslow Heath at this time included what is today Percy Road. Because permanent buildings were not allowed on the open Heath, James leased four fields from fellow Catholic, Lord Bellasis, who was then living in Whitton. A bake house, a granary, stables and a hospital were erected on fields now occupied by Whitton School, the Community Centre, Heathfield Library and St. Augustine's Church.

When William of Orange eventually landed at Brixham in Devon in November 1688, James fled abroad and the hospital fell into disuse. The field where the hospital was built is called the Hospital Field in the 1818 Twickenham Enclosure Award, which also contains an order for the building of a road from the present Nelson Road to cross Hospital Bridge over the River Crane towards Twickenham and Teddington. The general naming of the roads in Twickenham Parish took place in 1878, when Hospital Bridge Road came about.

Twickenham Cemetery next on Mr Giltrow's schedule was carved out of 4 acres of copyhold land in 1867. Like its Hounslow counterpart, it is minimally landscaped around the laying out of paths punctuated with yew, cypress and native trees. The twin Mortuary Chapels designed by Charles Jones are far less brooding and foreboding than their dour Gothic peers off the Hanworth Road, dressed as they are in stone similar to that of St Philip and St James church built five years earlier.

Among the few notable deceased rests Colonel Charles Edward Gostling-Murray, who died on 24 May 1892. As befitting his station in an age of unstinting deference, the band and 400 members of his Volunteer Regiment preceded the hearse from Whitton Park. The choir and orchestra of the Royal School of Music, Kneller Hall, attended the service, as well as an estimated 3,000 mourners. The Lodge we see today is later in date than the cemetery itself, but possibly the same as that occupied by Frederick Field on Census Night, 1901. The Sussex born Clerk to the Burial Ground had moved to Twickenham in 1884 with his wife, Amelia, taking over from James Alexander.

In 1891 the Fields were settled in Cemetery Lodge with their three children and Frederick's widowed mother. Ten year later and aged 42, Fredrick Field had become sexton and his eldest son, also called Frederick, the clerk. Arthur, the second son, was at a crossroads in his chosen career as an assistant in the Free Library Movement that had begun in Twickenham had begun in 1844. A Subscription Library and Reading Room were set up as a pioneering venture that lead to Twickenham claiming the distinction of becoming the first district in Middlesex (outside of London) to establish a Public Library. Two rooms of the Town Hall were made available stocked with 2,535 books. On 2nd October 1882 with Mr Charles S D Rabbitt in position as Librarian, the Reading Rooms were opened to the public. The Reference and Lending Departments came about a year later, and in a sample taken of readers using the new facility, a high proportion were 'artisans and labourers' aged between 15 and 30.

By the turn of the 20th century, the staff of the library included Arthur Field, the sexton's son at Twickenham Cemetery. The working and user conditions were poor. Inadequate lighting and ventilation, and the sheer lack of space saw an increasing need for a new, purpose built library, which would eventually come about in 1907 in Garfield Road. Despite even the massive development of the 1930s, Whitton would have to wait half a century for its own branch library. First, negotiations with the Selected Land and Property Co. Ltd., owners of the fast emerging Redway Estate, fell through and then in 1936 complications with other developers failed to acquire the eventual site of Heathfield Library.

Hanworth Lodge was considered in 1949, but its distance from the centre of the new town could not justify the scheme. Then in 1955, £10,778 was allocated the building of a library on the Hospital Bridge Road site, only to have the Minister of Housing recommend that the scheme should be deferred in the interests of 'retrenchment on capital expenditure'. However, following a successful appeal, Heathfield Library was eventually opened in 1960. Whitton School and the Community centre also appeared around this time together with provision for a new ward to be known as Heathfield.

The demanding style of St Augustine's church also has its roots in the 1930s as the process of urbanisation progressed. When the church of St. Philip & St. James was established in 1862, Whitton was taken out of the parish of Holy Trinity Twickenham. This was adequate for Whitton's meagre population for next six decades, but as the need for an additional church grew by 1935, so the London Diocesan Home Mission assigned a priest-in-charge to the church of St. Augustine of Canterbury. Services were at first held in the hall of the Bishop Perrin Memorial Church of England School, a voluntary school built further west along Hospital Bridge road in 1936. This parish was in turn taken out of St. Philip & St. James in 1951 to include all of Whitton south of the railway line. The foundation stone was laid on July 18 1957, and the new church opened the following year.

The church and its vicarage present a remarkable combination of the old and the new from an age when the building industry was responding to the economic pressures of a post-war Britain when greater reliance was placed more and more on factory-made materials and craftsmen's time was no longer cheap.

Individualism, romanticism and building styles were all as irrelevant from the mid-twentieth century as was the leaning towards the picturesque in the nineteenth. If St Augustine's style of architecture lies anywhere then it's in the Modern Movement that started with the traditionally motivated Arts and Crafts Movement suiting a need to simplify contemporary design. The whole is somewhat reminiscent of Sir Gilbert Scott's Bankside Power Station built between 1947 and 1963. To some, St Augustine's might appear brooding and uncompromising, whereas it is very much a traditional framework enhancing many period flavours into an almost brutally simple building, using traditional materials in a traditional way. The product of a highly rational and functional approach, its austerity is curiously more complete with the ubiquitous cellphone credo adorning the rigid geometry of its bold tower.

In 1901, nothing but open countryside greeted the eye of John Burridge Giltrow as he turned out of the cemetery gates and into Percy Road, then a narrow, hedge-trimmed country lane. On an earlier rural ride, it was William Cobbett who commented that all Middlesex is flat and ugly, and none less so than that from Richmond to Chertsey Bridge. Hounslow Heath he saw as but a sample of "all that is bad in soil and villainous in look...a fresh robbery of villages, hamlets, and farm labourers' buildings and abodes". W J Loftie, an antiquarian touring *In and Out of London* in 1873, likewise condemned the location as one "covered by an impenetrable veil. Rivers and ravines are masked, hills are levelled, marshes are hidden, a flood of brick fills up the hollows; the brooks run far underground. The flats are elevated, and the heights depressed".

John Burridge Giltrow would have been hard pressed to recognise such a place. At this point in his perambulations, H S Vaughn on his *Way About Middlesex* in 1893 recorded "quite a notable view for this part of the world. Looking eastward, the distant hills of Richmond are in sight and the Star and Garter conspicuous. Towards the north-east is Kneller Hall, picturesquely rising from the dark woods around Whitton...worthy of Constable's brush – a real piece of old England – stream, meadows and trees".

PERCY ROAD TO HOLLY BUSH CORNER

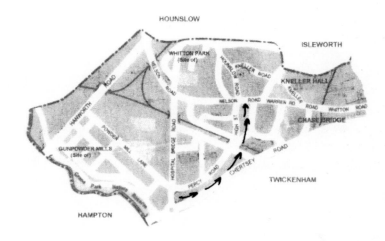

..........*Percy Road*.....

After some 300 yards along 'the main thoroughfare between Hounslow and Fulwell' (Percy Road), Mr Giltrow found the cemetery grounds giving way to three freehold enclosures of rich orchard land leased to Frank Peacock, the market gardener operating from Kneller Road. A clause in the lease allowed the landowner to resume possession for building or 'certain purposes' at four calendar months notice, with allowances made for losses incurred by the tenant, such as the value of growing crops. These three enclosures described in 1900 as 'affording a capital building estate' have indeed become 'profitably developed,' contained as they are in the 'long frontage to the Percy Road and to the Hospital Bridge' and, post 1930, Montrose Avenue.

The junction of Montrose Avenue with Percy Road is just visible centre left of this 1930s aerial view. At the railway bridge the countryside ends and Percy Road becomes the new High Street with the first clusters of housing starting to appear. The scar on the landscape (bottom right) heading in the direction of the High Street is Meadway, now curtailed by the A316 Great Chertsey Road taking the line of the tracks running through the orchards and arable land, partly in the holding of the 62-acre Jubilee Farm.

Before Mr Giltrow's enumeration Jubilee Farm was known as Warren Farm, a reference to when part of the land was reserved for breeding rabbits, once an important source of food on landed estates. In the 17th century Sir Robert Brett built a 'Warren House' on the higher ground close to Strathearn Avenue, where once a windmill stood. The change of name to Jubilee Farm came about as part of the celebrations marking Queen Victoria's Golden Jubilee in June 1887. It was leased in 1901 to Mr Poupart, a leading market gardener in the district, famous for his jam factory. Edward Pullen, his foreman, had moved with his wife, Leticia and their four children to the farm from Ealing after 1898.

The name of Warren Farm persisted, however. In 1903 a Mr Young asked the council for surplus gravel from the cemetery to be placed on "the Warren Farm footpath", which ran "across the field from Percy Road to the Staines Road", the original route from west Twickenham to Whitton Village. The request was denied, as was the call for the council to erect a gate at the point where the footpath met Percy Road, now Ross Road. At this spot today stands a building of no great historical value, except within the context of Whitton's evolving landscape.

Not immediately evocative of Wesleyan church building design in terms of simple classicism, nor a great Central Hall providing space for mass evangelism, or again nineteenth century Gothic with stained glass windows and transepts at the side, what we are presented with at this point is known as a Primitive Chapel with no embellishments to distract the worshippers. Built in 1952 in a good position along what had become established as a major thoroughfare, Whitton Methodist Church favours the pre and post-war years design of dual church halls, utilising a cross and table to provide the focal point symbolising the meeting of worship and daily life.

The chapel stands at the mouth of Ross Road, where the Warren Farm footpath once meandered northward at the time of Mr Giltrow's enumeration. Today housing estates and ultimately the A316 Great Chertsey road confound the original route. The Winning Post public house at the same time replaces the farmhouse, as it does the changes in design and use of the traditional public house. In its dining rooms, Art Deco fittings and lounge bars replaced the elaborate glass and brass and the more basic features of the traditional public bar.

Encompassing all of the moods and features of the 1930s with its exuberant use of curves, colour and streamlining, The Winning Post is instantly recognisable as the characteristic style of twentieth century architecture prompted by the growing popularity of other leisure venues, especially cinemas and dance halls that threatened the traditional pub position as the central social institution in most people's lives. Compared to Whitton's older drinking houses, The Winning Post represented a move upmarket, more respectable and attractive to the waves of incomers, where a man might take his wife out for the evening in a bright, glitzy and comfortable lounge environment.

Mr Giltrow fails to include Oxford Cottage, which stood north west of the Jubilee farmhouse towards Percy Road. Benjamin Leaver, another prominent market gardener and his sister, Elizabeth, who acted as his housekeeper, occupied it in 1891 when it was a census landmark. With no mention of it in Mr Giltrow's enumeration, he moved on next to The Grove, which nestled roughly between present day Pauline Crescent and Jubilee Avenue.

Man of means, Edward Gapp and his housekeeper, Sophia Owen, were resident in 1891. In 1901 Frederick Gapp headed the household. Given that Edward Gapp was aged 48 and single in 1891, and Frederick Gapp was 50 in 1901, the latter must have been a close relative, possibly a brother. Frederick was also a man of means. Under his roof lived his wife Elizabeth and his two stepsons, 29 year-old Arthur, also living on his own means who took the name of his adoptive father, whereas Edwin, an accountant's clerk, preferred to retain the family name of Haye-Johnson.

A stone set into the railway bridge leading into what is now the High Street, informs us that the structure Mr Giltrow crossed in 1901 was built in 1841. The bridge we cross today complements the station opened in July 1930, a pivotal point in Whitton's history, not only as the major catalyst in the district's transformation but also in the new town's identity. For had not the small population objected to the station being called West Twickenham, then the very name of Whitton might well have disappeared. The ancient village of Scrackidge, for example, lost its identity in favour of the more stylish Osterley.

High Street, Whitton.

Long before the trains stopped at Whitton there was no High Street, nor was there any other built structure recognisable today along the entire eastern flank running north from the new railway station. What we see today was before 1930 a continuation of Percy Road with a hedgerow containing fields and orchards as far as Twickenham.

The west side, however, had favoured some development for perhaps a century prior to Mr Giltrow's enumeration. If asked to describe the High Street today, then most observers would agree that it represents the quintessential 1930s shopping centre in its style and uniformity of composition. On closer inspection of the west side, however, the whole is made up of distinct blocks of piecemeal development, each ghosting the footprints of what went before.

Where Barclay's Bank today occupies the corner of the High Street and Constance Road originally stood numbers 1– 4 Hope & Anchor Cottages, a set of four-roomed dwellings facing south towards the railway line. Along Percy Road as far as 108, High Street were 1 – 4 Hume Cottages, and next to them as far as Boots were numbers 1 – 4 Notts Cottages. Between 94 High Street and the Tesco store stood 1 –5 Daisy Cottages. Woodbine Cottages next appear to have been three separate households each comprising just two rooms.

This aerial view of the Redway Estate under construction shows Percy Road entering the new town development from open countryside. Centre left of the railway station under construction, the first shops have appeared on the east side of the High Street.

The completed High Street looking south towards the station has changed very little. Barclays Bank today occupies the corner of the High Street and Constance Road. Boots (then 'The Chemist') is still in situ.

Thirty years earlier, Hope & Anchor Cottages occupied the site of Barclays Bank. At the time of Mr Giltrow's Enumeration number four was unoccupied. Frank Anstead in number three had moved to Whitton in 1890 when he was a railway platelayer. By 1901 he had improved his position to that of railway blacksmith. Living with him was his wife, Ann, a son and daughter and Frank's Father-in-law, 81-year-old Allan Pocock.

Gardener & florist James Ketchell had been living in one of these cottages since 1881 when he was recorded as the 15-year-old son of Stephen Ketchell, an agricultural labourer. Then his mother, Lucy, a laundress, was alive and he had a brother, George. Boarder, Henry Smith, a carman labourer, rented one of the four rooms. Living next door was Emily Hedges, also 15 and working as a domestic servant. By 1891 James and Emily were married with two young sons, Ernest aged two and George just four months. Ten years later and 12-year-old Ernest was living next door with his grandparents and with no sign of nine-year-old George. Eight-year-old Agnes was now the eldest child at home, followed by William and then Harry, aged four. Occupying the boarder's room was fellow florist, James Meapham.

Retired blacksmith, George Bennett was living in number one Hume Cottages in 1881 with his widowed daughter Eliza and her two sons, Leonard and Walter, aged 14 and 12 respectively and daughter Ada, aged 10, all of whom were born in Whitton. Only Ada remained at home in 1891 with her mother. She was aged 20 and with a three-year-old daughter, Mabel. Ada gave her marital status as single, which, given the strong social stigma surrounding illegitimacy in Victorian England, indeed deep into the 20th century, was a bold declaration.

'Loose women' were often kept away from others of their sex of good character in the workhouses. Sometimes an illegitimate child would be raised by grandparents or married relatives as the sister or nephew of the unwed mother. While the Victorians' heightened sense of social conscience recognized the need for reform, it wasn't until 1889 that the Prevention of Cruelty to Children Act came about, nine years after the establishment of the Royal Society for the Prevention of Cruelty to Animals.

Mabel's place of birth given as Torquay indicates a common discretion in sending the mother away to an area she was not known during her pregnancy. Otherwise Ada Bennett made no other pretence. In 1901 she gave her occupation as working in her own right as a sick nurse. Mabel was now 13.

In number two Hume Cottages, gardener Frederick Ward was a relative newcomer to this corner of Whitton, arriving before 1889, the year his wife Georgina gave birth to their daughter, Elizabeth. Joseph Franklin next door first appears in the 1881 census as the 15-year-old son of a Berkshire born agricultural labourer. Unrecorded in the census of 1891, he reappears in Mr Giltrow's enumeration occupying two rooms of the same cottage together with his wife Blanche. His occupation was now that of a bricklayer's labourer, possibly working for William Fitzwalter, living at 1, Hope & Anchor Cottages.

Thomas Bradley was another enduring figure living along Percy Road, occupying two rooms of number four Hume Cottages with his wife Mary. In 1881 he was working as a ground labourer, in 1891 as an agricultural labourer but 20 years on and the 70-year-old declared himself to be a pauper. Entered into the relevant column, John Burridge Giltrow described the old man's condition as oddly similar to that of another pauper living in the Parish, one William Bradley of number one Murray Cottage, Pearce's Road, possibly a relation. Both were of the same age and both had worked as agricultural labourers. William Bradley's complaint was given as a 'growth in intestines, while Thomas suffered from 'ulcerated bowels.'

Numbers 1-4 Notts Cottages formerly ran north from what is today 108 High Street. After 94, High Street and the Tesco store stood 1-5 Daisy Cottages. Then came Woodbine Cottages, which were three separate households, each comprising just two rooms. In the view of the High Street taken in the 1950s (overleaf), only the grocer's shop window in the right foreground survives as the single feature on the landscape recognisable to John Burridge Giltrow from his enumeration in 1901.

In number four Notts Cottages, Mr Giltrow found another pair of paupers, 70-year-old Charles Pearce and his wife, Eliza. Both were born in Whitton in the 1830s and had been living along Percy Road at least since 1881 when together with their eldest daughter, 18-year-old Alice, they were all working as gardeners' labourers. Of the three other children, only the youngest, George aged 27, was at home in 1901 and working as a bricklayer's labourer.

At number three, Mr Giltrow recorded a rare sighting of a Whitton-based employee at the Gunpowder Mills, Richard Steptoe, although his job description is sadly indecipherable. With the room, or rooms, to spare there were two boarders, 56-year-old Richard Brown, a Navy pensioner, and 71 one-year-old widow Harriet Elmes who may well have lived in the same cottage since 1870. For in 1881 agricultural labourer John Elms was head of the household in an unnamed cottage on Percy Road. Harriet was then 54 and the mother of their four children, James, George, Sarah and the youngest, William, who was born in Whitton in 1870. In 1891 Harriet was now a widow living with her daughter Sarah and granddaughter, Edith Simms.

Occupying the four rooms of 2, Notts Cottages, was general labourer, Richard Hewitt, another Whitton born man, married to Mary and with a four-year-old son, also called Richard and their two-year-old daughter, Charlotte. Elizabeth Peck next door at number one was born in Whitton to John and Ann Peck in 1878, and followed by siblings Sidney, Florence and Emeline. Come 1901 and Elizabeth had left, Willie and Nellie had been born, and Sidney was working as an agricultural labourer like his father.

Numbers 1 –5 Daisy Cottages may well have been as new to the Whitton landscape in 1901 as were their incumbents compared to most of the neighbourhood. Arthur Leggins occupying number five was a 45-year-old Coventry born night watchman. His wife, Martha hailed from Somerset and their 15-year-old son, Herbert, working as a clerk, was born in Notting Hill. Ernest Payne, a railway servant born in Vauxhall lived next door in number four with his wife, Georgina, who was born in Westminster. Their three-year-old daughter, also called Georgina, was born in Eastleigh in Hertfordshire. Twenty-six year old carpenter William Hamilton, the head of the household at number three was born in neighbouring Feltham, his wife Rose in Hertfordshire and their nine-month-old son, George, in Whitton. Next door lived 38-year-old Hampstead born shop glass fitter Albert Jones, his wife Elizabeth, their nine-year-old daughter, Jennie and three-year-old son, George.

When Albert Jones was his son's age, poor quality plate glass was still produced using the crown glass process that involved spinning a large glass sphere to produce a large disc, which, when cool, was cut into a square. Its centre, or bull, was originally regarded as waste or a poor second and is now considered synonymous with Victorian period shop window detail. By the time Albert Jones entered his trade, mechanisation was producing cheap but imperfect window glass. He would have needed to reach his centenary before learning of the Pilkington Glass Company's invention of the float glass process that made possible vast shop windows and the limitless glass monoliths of the 1960s.

Completing the short run of Daisy Cottages was Leopold Butler, a 27-year-old railway clerk from Aldershot and his Cornish wife, Emma, living in number one. In number one Woodbine Cottages, 75-year-old garden labourer Peter Snell shared his meagre space with 58-year-old Ann Alden, variously described in previous censuses as a garden woman and as a servant. Sixty-six year old Irish born widow, Johanna Murphy, lived next door and after her came 65-year-old agricultural labourer, Robert Wilson and his wife, Sarah, both born in Hounslow. Possibly by 1901 some remedial work had taken place on these properties, as they now had three habitable rooms.

Both John Brennan and his wife Kate living in number three were born in Ireland and had been living in Twickenham at least since 1893 when their daughter Annie was born. Assuming that he was working in his declared profession at the time, the only sources of employment for John Brennan as a museum porter in 1901 were all situated in London. Locally there had been a technical museum provided by Thomas Twining, which was opened in Twickenham in 1860 but destroyed by fire eleven years later and not rebuilt. In 1896, the Duc d'Orleans maintained a private collection at York House, which was acquired in 1906 by its last private owner, Sir Ratan Tata, the Indian merchant Prince who was also a great collector. Kingston, as the oldest established museum locally opened in the same year. If John Brennan did commute daily to London, then he would have taken advantage of the special workingmen's fares introduced onto the railways to supply labour into the growing capital.

At number two Woodbine Cottages, Mr Giltrow recorded a second employee at the Gunpowder Mills, 38-year-old James George, a tin worker originally from Heston. Annie, his wife was born nearby in Sunbury, and their three daughters each under the age of six were all born in Twickenham. In 1891, agricultural labourers Robert and Ann Wilson were living at number three. Ten years later and Robert (aged by just two years) was living at number one without Ann, but like Peter Snell, with his own servant, 65-year-old Mary Roak. Applethorpe Lodge, listed as an afterthought by John Burridge Giltrow, was unoccupied and stood about where number 80 High Street is today.

North of a one and a half-acre field ending where Tranmere Road emerges into the High Street today, were numbers 1 – 2, Thomas Villas. Immediately beyond and where today a charmless slab of 1960s decorated concrete mantles the Iceland supermarket and other business premises, stood 1 –2 Neville Cottages (or Nevells Place). Next, were the curiously named Odd Manns Cottages and nestling between them and the Admiral Nelson (the large building in the distance) were numbers 1 –2 Nelson Cottages.

At home at 2, Thomas Villas on the night of Sunday 31st March 1901 were Wiltshire born Thomas Farmer, his Heston born wife, Emma, their seven-year-old niece Emma George and two boarders, farm labourers Jamie Bacon and Henry King who was born in Whitton in 1850. Oxfordshire born market garden labourer, John Wheeler occupied number one Thomas Villas, together with his wife Elizabeth and their 19-year-old daughter, Ellen, who was born in Whitton and working as a domestic servant. Sons Harry and Charles were both dairymen labourers. Elizabeth Wheeler was born in Oxfordshire in 1850 and gave her occupation as that of char-woman. John aged nine and six-year old Margaret completed the Wheeler household.

Neville Cottages, or Nevells Place, was where Samuel Brister had been running his grocery business for at least 20 years prior to Mr Giltrow's enumeration. Born in Whitton in 1852, he married Laura before 1873 when the first of their eight children, Jane, was born. On Census Night, 1901, Jane was not recorded. Twenty-six year old dressmaker Gertrude was now the eldest at home. Alexander at age 24 had progressed from milk boy ten years earlier to working on his own account with his father as a Greengrocer. Like her elder sister, 22-year-old Ellen is not included in Mr Giltrow's enumeration and no occupation is recorded for Kate at age 18. Mary, at the ripe old age of 15 was still at school, as were her younger siblings, Annie, Cordelia and Stanley.

In the adjoining house lived 54-year-old Oxfordshire born general labourer, George Reeves, his Whitton born wife Mary and their three children. Charlie, the eldest, was a general labourer like his father and was born in Whitton 20 years earlier. His brother Samuel was a carter and their 14-year-old sister Rose had typically left the schoolroom behind her to work as a general servant. Her world was poles apart from the girl next door enjoying the relative affluence afforded by her shopkeeper father.

In 1901 the class system was no longer neatly divided up into the upper, middle, and working classes. In Whitton, the days of the local landed elite might have ended, but the grinding poverty of working-class life remained. It was in the ranks of the growing middle classes, which included office workers, factory foremen, teachers, travelling salesmen and small businessmen that had changed the most. As a retail shopkeeper, Samuel Brister would have generally enjoyed a good deal of importance in the community. He was more likely to be literate, though not necessarily well educated. He would go through life with a more confident and less deferential air. Importantly, he would also be more likely to have a Parliamentary vote, with influence on the state of the nation. Locally, his attitude could be expressed as to any expenditure out of the rates by becoming involved with the local government boards or bodies such as vestries and boards of guardians.

His business (pictured above in the early 1960s) would not have competed with local farmers and growers for fruit and vegetables. Locals would have been able to purchase them direct or at a weekly market, the mainstay of the poorest classes and where they could haggle over prices. Samuel Brister might well have preferred to take receipt of orders from the better class of customer, offering a 'High Class' service to those occupying the villas and larger private houses in the area, but he wouldn't have been in a position to disenfranchise the poor literally living on his doorstep and so would have sold quantities of produce to suit all pockets.

In times of unemployment or sickness, or when the weekly housekeeping was exhausted, goods might be supplied on credit. However, once in debt it was extremely difficult for the poor to get out. Mostly, it was virtually impossible for the majority of working class families to survive on a single wage alone. In consequence, it was often the case that both partners worked, and so did their children as soon as they were of age.

A typical working class combined family income in 1901 was around £2 a week, or £100 a year. A male Agricultural Labourer who was married earned in today's terms about £1.30 a week, sometimes with rent-free accommodation, coals and other advantages. Unmarried men and boys earned about half that amount with their keep. Rose Reeves' earnings as a domestic servant would have been as little as £10 or £12 per year. Provided her father and brother found work for at least two-thirds of the year, the total annual household income might have been less than £100. Samuel Brister, the Green Grocer next door earned double that amount.

In the first of the two Odd Mann Cottages, Mr Giltrow found 40-year-old spinster Phillis Nevell living on her own means. In 1891 she was recorded as a dressmaker and living with her mother, Emma and Father Peter, a builder and carpenter. Probability related to the publican of the Admiral Nelson and others in the area variously listed as Nevell, Nevill or Nevells, Phillis was born in one of the cottages in 1861. Presumably conditions were comfortable enough, as were those of her 73 year-old widowed neighbour, Ann Eden, living in the second Odd Mann's Cottage.

Nelson Cottages, however, were less savoury, condemned by the Inspector of Nuisances as being 'without sufficient water closet; earth closet or privy accommodation'. By 1901, notices were increasingly placed on landlords for the supply of water to flush the toilets to be connected to the Water Board's main supply and to fix all the necessary domestic pipes, cisterns and draw-off taps to update the 'privy' situated at the bottom of the garden. Faecal matter was contained in a vault. Often these chambers were not properly covered over and the arrangement for their regular emptying was sporadic.

Wastewater was drained into a cesspool, often half the distance to the house. Sometimes the waste from the sink was connected directly to the vault, which, if overflowing, returned waste matter directly into the house. It was not uncommon for two or more vaults to be connected by means of an overflow drain into a cesspool, the exact location of which was only discovered when the overload made itself known under pressure.

Leaving agricultural labourer Arthur Fisher and his wife Charlotte to the misfortunes of 2, Nelson Cottages, John Burridge Giltrow passed by the more modest Admiral Nelson of his day for the last stage of his enumeration. Looking east, Nelson Road carried round in a wide arc northwards to Whitton village. A high brick wall containing market garden land ran along its southern length. Kneller Hall was then the dominant feature on the horizon, free of the rooftops framing much the same view today.

NELSON ROAD (EAST) TO KNELLER ROAD

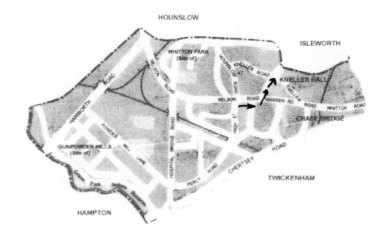

.....Nelson Road to Mr Mann's Inclusive.'

Apart from the surviving buildings comprising Holly Bush Corner, the only built structure recognisable to John Burridge Giltrow at this point in his enumeration would have been the modest relic now 122, Nelson Road and turned over to offices.

This may have once taken the name of King's Cottage from George King, a Berkshire born carman labourer who was located in the vicinity in 1880, the year his son James was born. Alfred Cutt was the tenant when Mr Giltrow called to record him, his wife, Louisa and their five children. West Cottage next on Mr Giltrow's schedule disappeared in 1906 to make way for the Edwardian terrace we see today. Five years earlier, Hanworth born soldier Henry Goddard was living in one room with his wife Caroline. Occupying another room was 60-year-old Eliza Griffiths, a cook who married gardener Charles Griffiths who was head of the household in 1881 and sub-letting another room to lodger Mansell Scott. At the time of Mr Giltrow's enumeration Eliza was now renting her room from Lydia Brown who occupied West Cottage's two other rooms.

Lydia Brown previously lived in one of the neighbouring Anderson Cottages with her husband George and their two unmarried sons, Richard aged 36 and Jesse, 33. By 1891, Lydia was a widow. Richard was still living her, as was seven-year-old granddaughter confusingly called Mabel Young. Blacksmith's labourer, James Brown, occupied the other Anderson's Cottage. He, like Lydia, was also born in Twickenham, but there appears to be no family connection. Sometime before 1901 James Brown secured tenancy of both cottages, perhaps to accommodate his new business, that of whitesmith; a craftsman working in tin, brass or bronze or other light metals, either polishing finished work or producing ornaments and jewellery and household metalwork.

Anderson's Cottages were located on what is today the corner of Prospect Crescent and Nelson Road. In Mr Giltrow's day there was no Prospect Crescent. The only built structure on the landscape towards Whitton village was the pair of solidly built, isolated dwellings, more in keeping with 19th century railway or cemetery architecture in their construction and design. Today they comprise 84 and 86 Nelson Road.

165

With their coat of hard wearing yellow stock bricks, black slate roofs and carved stone lintels, clearly, these were buildings specifically designed to withstand an exposed situation. Today they retain their air of remoteness, thoroughly disconnected from the neighbouring 1920s bungalows (allegedly built by James Wills for each of his daughters) and 1930s shops.

A local estate agent once claimed that these buildings were former hunting lodges belonging to the Whitton Park Estate. Although hunting was never a feature at Whitton, the buildings were indeed lodges, built around 1850 when the estate was reunited. Others along Nelson Road included Wells Cottage towards the railway bridge and South Lodge on the corner of Hounslow and Nelson Roads. The more elaborate Gostling Villa opposite The White Hart in Kneller Road was perhaps home to the head gardener or the estate manager in overall charge of daily management. After these came the flower and vegetable gardeners. The third class of person in the estate hierarchy was domestic servants and labourers. It was invariably the dedication of the estate workers that would have ensured productivity and so tended to be treated reasonably well.

Colonel Gostling-Murray died a year after the census of 1891 when the lodges along this stretch of Nelson Road were recorded as Gosling's Cottages. Then, one of the occupants was reported 'Away from Home.' In the adjoining dwelling lived 71-year-old Whitton-born Elizabeth West and her son Edwin who was a coachman like his father before him. His wife Mary worked as a laundress. The couple may well have been among the last to serve the family at The Big House before the Estate's decline.

In 1901, Stephen West, a 55-year-old retired police constable occupied the cottage, now recorded as 2, Nelson Villas, with his wife and three children. Carl Fiestler, a 46-year-old market garden clerk was occupying number one with his wife, Mary and their two daughters, Gertrude and Alice, having moved from London to Hounslow in 1889, the year their son George was born. Both Carl and Mary were born in Germany and retained their nationality.

The first stage of Edwardian development along this section of Nelson Road was taking place as John Burridge Giltrow passed by a narrow strip of land that would eventually become the eastern spur to Prospect Crescent. A few months after his enumeration and St Joseph's Villas would be ready for occupation. The small business premises attaching (pictured to right below) appears to have been selling prints or pictures when this photograph was taken in about 1905.

Bicycles were repaired here for as long as people can remember and before the days of domestic electrical supply where lead-acid batteries, or accumulators, would be taken for re-charging in order to enjoy the novelty of a new-fangled entertainment called the wireless. Today, the property is a hairdressing salon, one of many that seem to flourish in Whitton. Fashionable hairstyles in Mr Giltrow's day were limited to the middle and upper classes. Working men and women carried out the task periodically at home as required, rather than regularly. A shave could be had for one penny at Dove's the barber in Hounslow High Street. The better off often had access to a personal set of seven razors labelled Sunday to Saturday. King Camp Gillette invented the disposable blade in America in 1895. Ten years later when the Gillette razor came to Britain, sales had risen from 168 blades in the first years to a staggering 2.5 million.

Whereas all other references to him have been erased, numbers 1 –5 Kyezor Terrace (now 52-60 Nelson Road) retains the name of the German philanthropist who 'drove the heathen out' and earned himself the title 'King of Whitton'. Built for the working poor by Louis Kyezor in the 1860s, what was originally number five (left) underwent a change of use in 1914 when Mrs E James made an application for it to become a fish frying business.

This was agreed subject to adequate ventilation, proper arrangements for cleaning fish and the type of cooking stove, waste receptacles to be used and appropriate flooring. The first Fish & Chip shop opened in London, in 1860 and in Mossley near Oldham, Lancashire, three years later. The trade expanded hugely amongst the growing industrial population of Great Britain after the development of the steam trawler, which brought in fish from all over the North Atlantic, and the railways that ensured fish were swiftly distributed to every part of the United Kingdom. The trade thrived especially at holiday resorts where people could enjoy standard fare familiar in households irrespective of which part of the country they came from.

Ten months before Census Night 1901, the Medical Health Officer had reported this same dwelling and neighbouring number four to be unsafe and unfit for human habitation. The borough surveyor was advised to inspect and report with a view to taking steps under the Housing of the Working Classes Act to obtain a closing order. On 3rd September 1900, the Surveyor recommended serving notice on the owner of both premises to bring the properties up to the proper condition. The initial work was deemed to be unsatisfactory, but with no more reports after 17th September, we must assume that these dwellings were more wholesome when Mr Giltrow called.

Then, general labourer William Young, a 77-year-old Whitton man was in occupation with his wife, Eliza, 29 years his junior. Their eldest boys Alfred and Henry were a bricklayer's labourer and general carman respectively. Twelve year-old Tilly would soon be old enough to work. Meanwhile she would have been expected to help her mother around the house and to look after her younger brother and sister, Frederick and Elsie.

Occupying number four, Kyezor Terrace was Whitton-born John Ashton, his wife Mary and their three young children. John Ashton was also a bricklayer's labourer, an increasingly familiar occupation throughout 1901 Whitton, offering evidence of urbanisation beginning to reach out from the directions of Twickenham and Hounslow. Twenty-nine year old Charles Ash was a general carter, also born in Whitton and who filled number three Kyezor Terrace with himself, his wife, Elizabeth, their five children, his brother-in-law, William Jury, his wife Elizabeth and their two infant daughters. As well as the issue of chronic overcrowding, the four-roomed cottage was also found to be in a very dirty condition with notice served on the owner to have it whitewashed and cleansed.

Similarly number two, occupied by general carman Stephen Benn, his wife Annie and the couple's seven children. The eldest boy, also called Stephen, declared an occupation tinged with irony given the name attaching the terrace where he lived. For not only had Louis Kyezor been responsible for providing the roof over his head, but also, in part, the promotion of the boy's living.

In 1868 Louis Kyezor was an elected member of the Twickenham Local Board, which took many local government affairs away from the Vestry. Of his many proposals for Whitton was included an additional five street lamps, with a person appointed to light and clean them. His last act as a member of the board before his murder a year later was to propose two additional lamps for the village, one by the Admiral Nelson and one at the White Hart.

Little had changed by 1901 when a large number of Whitton residents were complaining to the Lighting Committee about the dangerous state of the roads at night, especially at the upper end of Nelson Road between Hospital Bridge Road and Hanworth Road. Responding promptly to their concerns, the Brentford Gas Company provided for an additional three lamps and a new wrought iron column complete with directional plates installed at the junction of Hounslow and Kneller Roads. Meanwhile, 15-year-old Stephen Benn, as Whitton's sole recorded lamplighter, would set out each day at sunset with his ladder used reach the lamps in their glass enclosures. With a 'U' shaped metal rod he would switch on the gas, which was ignited by a lit taper. At around 5.a.m. he would be up and about with his ladder, taking the same route, this time to extinguish the lights and clean the glass.

The new-fangled concept of electricity was greeted with suspicion. In January 1900, the council turned down a request from the Richmond Electric Light and Power Company Ltd. to supply electric light to the district. A year later the Edmundson's Electricity Corporation Ltd. started building their power station in the district, but gas remained the preferred form of power for decades to come. In 1931, of the 1,000 new lamps planned for Twickenham borough, just 205 were converted to electricity.

The Electricity Act of 1947 dissolved the London and Home Counties Joint Electricity Authority to create the South Eastern Electricity Board, by which time electric clocks and automatic ignition replaced the men who set out at each sunset and sunrise with their ladders. Stephen Benn would have been into his eighties and beginning to take for granted leaps in technology such as television when the last gas lamps disappeared from the streets of Whitton.

Bricklayer Joseph Ashton, his wife and two small children living at number one Kyezor Terrace were spared the cramped conditions next door to them at number five, which were but as nothing compared to residents occupying 1-5 Manns Cottages, a huddle of multi-occupancy households located in what is today a builders yard behind 50 and 50a Nelson Road. Here, the appalling living conditions endured by seasonal workers echoed the shocking experience of Louis Kyezor when he first came to the village in the 1840s.

In the summer of 1900, the Inspector of Nuisances recommended a closing order on 2, Mann's Cottages as unsafe and unfit for human habitation. Numbers 2a and 3a were in a filthy condition, requiring whitewashing and cleaning. The cesspools were full in two of the other cottages, but the owners held out, making repeated requests for the works to be adjourned until after the harvest. Following five summonses and fines imposed of 20 shillings per house plus costs and court fees, the Medical Health Officer was able to report that remedial work was progressing satisfactorily. However, the five units would eventually grow to eight and conditions deteriorate to such an extent that they would all be cleared in 1914.

When John Burridge Giltrow called by, market garden labourer Jesse Corrington was occupying a newly cleansed 1, Manns Cottages with his wife, May, who was born in Ireland. She had spent some time in India where her 21-year-old son by a previous marriage, Charles Gaffney, was born. General labourers Francis and Bridget Atkin headed the household of number two, then Frederick and Sophia Thompson with their son, also called Frederick, and in number four was 71-year-old widow, Sarah Ashton, who had moved out of the more salubrious four-roomed roadside accommodation comprising number 5 Manns Cottages after 1891. In 1901, James Lindsay, a 48-year-old house painter was in occupation together with wife, Eliza, and their four children. The building was probably no architectural gem, but it would have represented a far healthier alternative to the hovels at its rear. A bland, 1960s former office space numbering 50 and 50a Nelson Road now occupies the site.

Edging his way further north along Nelson Road, Mr Giltrow failed to include in his enumeration the earliest example of architecture celebrating, albeit a muted history of nonconformity in Whitton, The Gospel Hall.

The first recorded meeting of Nonconformists in Whitton took place in 1829 in a house occupied by a William Geary. The London City Mission, already active in the district, focused on Whitton in the late 1830s, and in 1844 a group of independents met in a house, which stood virtually opposite the site of the Gospel Hall. Census Sunday 1851 included the first and only official census undertaken to determine church attendance, which demonstrated little appetite for dissent in the Twickenham district. Undeterred, the London City Mission began meetings at the newly built Whitton School in 1857.

As interest grew, so the Avenue Baptist Church was built in St Margarets and in 1881 the Gospel Hall in Whitton, both daughter churches of Twickenham Baptist Church. When the Avenue Church made way for the new A316 Great Chertsey Road in the 1930s, the Trustees used the money to buy land opposite The Prince Albert on Hounslow Road. When the church was opened in April 1935, the Gospel Hall became surplus to requirements.

An opportunity arose for the council to acquire it for use as a branch library for Whitton, but despite the attractive asking price of £850 attention was focused on the creation of a new London Borough of Twickenham Borough and so the opportunity was lost. Whitton acquired its first library on 16th December 1940 at numbers 64 -66, High Street, where it remained until 1946 when it moved to numbers 38-40. In 1973 the current facility set behind the Admiral Nelson was built. The Gospel Hall was eventually sold and is now occupied by a flooring company.

Mr Giltrow called next on 'The Shop', which occupied the gap we see today between the Gospel Hall and 1960s maisonettes. Although specialist retailers were yet to find a niche in 1901 Whitton, grocers and general dealers had doubled over the past decade with the arrival of general dealer George Davison from Feltham where his two children, Thomas, aged 13 and Jessie, a year younger, were born. Next to his establishment was James Holt, who traded as grocer and postmaster.

As the anti-penultimate location of Whitton's peripatetic Post Office, the business had shifted from Elizabeth Allenson's cottage on Kneller Road sometime after 1891, emphasising the decline in the family fortunes begun by her father in 1848. In sharp contrast were the lives of James Holt's two daughters, Charlotte who was born in Nottingham in 1878 and 16-year-old sister, Lillian, who was born in Hounslow like her younger brother, Augustus. In 1901 both girls were working as a Post Office counter clerks when the most common work for women remained domestic service.

The lifestyle with its accommodation, food and regular wages was far preferable to the backbreaking grind of the factory or seasonal work in the fields. But at the dawn of the new century, popular journals and magazines were publishing stories and articles about the 'new woman' with a job, riding a bicycle and smoking cigarettes. Charlotte and Lillian Holt no longer required a chaperone. They were independent-minded, preferring their white-collar job as clerks to that of a life of toil answerable to a domineering male. By 1901, the proportion of female clerks had risen steadily to include new businesses, such as the Post Office.

But while it was recognised that within a certain range of duties women did the work more effectively, they were paid less than their male counterparts and a woman was required to resign her position when she married, thus reducing the numbers on the pension list. As well as holding positions such as counter staff, women were also employed in the new technologies of telegraphy and telephony.

The previously privately owned inland Telegraph system was transferred to the State in 1870, when The Post Office took over a service with 1,058 telegraph offices generating some seven million telegrams transmitted per annum. Moving on to expand the UK telegraph network to rural areas previously commercially unattractive to the private companies, the Superintendent Engineer of the Post Office wrote to Twickenham council on 10 October 1899, asking for permission to begin the process of laying underground pipes in the District.

1884 saw the birth of public call offices, which any member of the public could use. Known as silence cabinets, the first accessible to people living in Whitton was installed in Richmond Town Hall in 1890. Freestanding Call Offices (later called Telephone Kiosks) were also around by this time in the form of small wooden huts where a three-minute call could be made for two old pennies. Some had a coin box built into them, while others had an attendant to collect the fee.

Behind the premises of Messrs Davison and Holt were 1 and 2, Retreat Cottages, both of which had escaped the attention of the Inspector of Nuisances prior to Mr Giltrow's visit. Two months later and notices were served on the pair of them to be whitewashed and thoroughly cleansed. Enduring, or immune, to the conditions of these four-roomed dwellings on Census Night was Whitton-born Frederick and Hannah Alder and their five children who occupied number two. Like the majority of his immediate neighbours, Frederick Alder was a market garden labourer, as were his older sons, Frederick and Herbert. David Donaghue, a 49-year-old market garden labourer who had arrived in Whitton before February 1901 when his baby son, Joseph, was born, headed the household of number one.

Deviating from the path of previous enumerators, Mr Giltrow next crossed over to the east side of Nelson Road to make for the 'short cut', which today runs beside 77 Nelson Road. Before 1930 there was no Warren Road. To get to Twickenham from the direction of Holly Bush Corner, heavier traffic was forced to take the convoluted route via Kneller Road. Lighter carts and pedestrians took the short cut, which still leads towards the old Married Quarters enclosure and onto Warren Road (below).

Hereafter the unwholesome tang of poverty gave way to hints of blossom. Stretching from what is today Hall Farm Drive as far west as Holly Bush corner was a brick wall wired with the clipped stems of peach and nectarine. Rows of raspberries and loganberries vied with fruit trees under cropped with strawberries or winter cabbages and cauliflowers, depending on the season. The roses, hard pruned, awaited the promise of peonies and chrysanthemums starting to show with the narcissi and daffodils ready to be cut. Although Kent had all but superseded Middlesex as the garden of England, there would be plenty of work to be had in these fields well into the 20th century.

Farmer and market gardener Walter Mann appears on the List of Men qualified to serve as Jurors in Twickenham for September 1864. In 1881 he and his wife, Charlotte, were occupying 70 acres of land south of Warren Road, employing 16 men, eight women and one boy. The eldest daughter, also called Charlotte, was born in Brentford in 1861, as was the eldest son, Walter, a year later. His younger brother, James, was born in Whitton in 1865, as was his sister Eliza three years later. The youngest child, Lewis, was born in 1879.

Warren Farm isn't named in the census returns before 1891. Charlotte Mann was in that year a widow and living at The Warren with Charlotte, Walter, James, Eliza and 10-year-old Frederick. Lewis, who would have now been aged 12, fails to make an appearance. In 1901 Charlotte Mann was 66 years old and living on her own means with her daughter Charlotte and son Frederick in The Croft. Warren Farm was in the hands of 36-year-old James Mann. His wife Mary was from Ireland and they had two daughters, 14-year-old Miriam and six year old Mary. Twenty-three year old Matilda Backland from Longford in Middlesex worked as their domestic servant.

The Warren was by now was partially ruinous, with only four rooms habitable occupied by market garden labourer, William Herbert, his wife, Emma and their six children. Charlotte Mann had submitted a building application for additions to the house in 1900, which was not recommended. When Warren Road came about in 1931, The Warren and Warren Farm were swept away and with them any associated relics of the first great houses to be built in Whitton. No records exist for Whitton before 1219, but in a document dated 20th July 1480 and again in another dated 1609, reference is made to a large house with a courtyard. A second and larger house was built between 1619 and 1622 between Hall Farm Close and The Ridge.

The Ridge is a somewhat ambiguous choice of name within the context of a landscape dismissed for centuries by writers and antiquarians as 'flat, monotonous and uninteresting to a degree'. A ridge is by definition a long narrow hilltop or range, a feature it took the keen eye of one 20th century developer or local authority official to fully appreciate in reading this landscape.

At this point the land lies 60 to 70 feet above the datum line on the edge of the Lynch Hill Terrace, one of a series in the Thames valley cut through by fast-flowing rivers depositing and transporting sands and gravels throughout eleven glacial and interglacial cycles. The highest points on these levels are the most ancient and the lowest the most recent. Twickenham is settled on the lowest of these, the Taplow Terrace. The ridge of the Lynch Hill Terrace extends in an arc southeast towards Hampton and northeast towards Hounslow, suggesting an ancient ridge road. 'Whit' in Anglo-Saxon refers to the bend of a river or a winding geological feature. 'Ton' can describe a sandy hillock, or a dune, hence Whit-ton.

Ralph Treswell's Chart of 1607 shows a house due west of The Ridge to be in the occupation of 'Mr Suckling,' yet to be knighted for his services to both James and Charles 1. Highly ambitious, he accumulated property in Whitton and many other parts of the country during his time in the lucrative post of Comptroller to the Royal Household. He was knighted in 1616, seven years after his son, also called John, was born in Whitton. The latter, an inveterate gambler, man-about-court and soldier, established himself as a poet and was knighted by King Charles 1. In 1640 he was involved in the Army plot to restore the power of the King over Parliament and to free the Earl of Strafford from the Tower of London. Discovery led to his flight to France where he was either murdered by his valet or died by his own hand in 1642. The house had fallen into decay by 1730 and the land was leased out as farmland until the 1930s. The Ridge, as it became known 30 years after Mr Giltrow's day, was for years the subject of a hotly contested public rights of way issue.

Alfred and Eliza Woodward and their two sons, 24-year-old William and 20-year-old Arthur arrived in Whitton from Kensington in 1880. They ran an 8 acre market garden business between Hall Farm Drive and The Ridge until some time before 1891 when the younger son, Arthur, now married and with a growing family of his own, had moved to Woodward Cottage on Kneller Road where the offending trackway began and survives between the rear of the Duke of Cambridge and 99 Kneller Road (overleaf).

By 1901, Arthur Woodward had moved again, to Whitton Dean Farm. The Woodwards could therefore lay claim to living close or beside the footpath for 20 years. If its historic provenance lay anywhere, then it was with the Sucklings. Glover's Map of 1635 shows a length of trackway taking the line of The Ridge south from their property towards Hospital Bridge Road. Although the Woodwards had no legal claim on any part of it, it was the duty of the district council under the Local Government Act 1894 to protect all rights of way. These included footways, horseways, or packways, primeways and cartways, none of which categorised that which had unofficially become known as Woodward's Footpath. The police didn't patrol the route nor did the highway authority maintain it, so the council required evidence in the form of witness statements that there was a prima facie case for a right of way created either by custom or dedication. In his evidence, Arthur Woodward declared that to the best of his knowledge, the footpath had never been a public right of way, except for persons working on his farm. There had been gates, which were locked infrequently, mostly to move the cows down the lane towards pasture.

Like Mr Mann at The Warren, Arthur Woodward knew of no Whitton folk who used the lane, 'only strangers coming up the slip from the village'. Mr Benjamin Leaver, who took on Jubilee Farm in 1889, disagreed. Dogs had been exercised along the footpath for decades, he maintained. Strawberry pickers for both Mr Mann senior and junior entered the footpath from Percy Road, past Jubilee Cottage and into Mr Manns' land, then past Mr Woodward's farm and garden without interruption towards Mr Young's Farm at Whitton Dean. George Scorell, another witness, once travelled the footpath without hindrance with the late Mr George Baker, the Manor Reeve of Twickenham.

Others submitting evidence to the footpath inquiry, argued that 'before Percy Road took on its more modern formation', the footpath was traditionally the most direct and shortest bridle path from Twickenham to Whitton village. In his Memorials of Twickenham, the Rev R S Cobbett noted that in 1820 the owner of the linseed oil mills by Hospital Bridge denied public access to the footpath, but was ordered to reopen it. Other witnesses pointed to the use of the footpath as an accommodation road over the railway track for any purpose of cartage and farm workforce. Mr W Bishop, Solicitor of the London & South Western Railway Company hesitantly confirmed an 'Occupation Lane' numbered 115 in the Parish of Twickenham where the railway line was on a slight embankment, thus necessitating a footbridge.

This, however, was purely an accommodation and not a public right of way issue as the lands were copyhold to the Manor of Isleworth Syon. William Anderson of Holly Bush Corner made it clear that the bridge was there to save having a level crossing on account of the danger. He had only been along the path a dozen or so times since 1889 with his gun and was never threatened. Despite a huge amount of time and effort expended on the inquiry, the matter was never resolved.

Today, Ross Road opposite Twickenham cemetery is where the footpath cut off from Percy Road. The road bridge over the A316 Chertsey road now replaces the railway footbridge. Bridge Way and Redway Drive interrupt the direct route towards The Ridge and Warren Road after which the fragment of footpath survives towards Kneller Road.

Re-emerging back into the village via the short cut, Mr Giltrow resumed his enumeration with numbers 1 and 2, Postman's Rest, a pair of four-roomed cottages located in the rear garden of what is now 77 Nelson Road. Possibly their name suggests they once served in some capacity the rural Letter Carriers who had to travel longer distances than their urban colleagues collecting and delivering mail. Mr Giltrow recorded Mary Clement, a 62-year-old widow, occupying one of the cottages with her son Jesse and his brother William, 19 years his junior. In the neighbouring cottage was 26-year-old Walter Greenbank from Bermondsey and his Heston-born wife, Martha. The words 'shoeing' and 'horse' escaping the flamboyant slash of the census clerk's tally mark, it's reasonable to assume a family relationship with that of Harry Greenbank who was living and working nearby at The Forge.

Another misdemeanour vexing the Inspector of Nuisances in the immediate wake of Mr Giltrow's enumeration was the question of these and other properties being without a dustbin. 'Dustmen' at that time exactly matched their job description in so far as they mostly collected the ash from coal fires, which they took to dust yards where men, women and children worked on the heaps as scavengers, sieving the breize or course particles for use as a soil conditioner and for brick making. Materials such as glass and metal were returned to merchants. In 1890 the British Paper Company was established specifically to make paper and board from recycled materials obtained from organisations such as the Salvation Army and rag-and-bone men. The process of waste regulation started the evolution in local authority power, ruling that householders were required to keep their waste in a 'movable receptacle', or bin, which the local authorities were required to empty every week. A charge could be made for every day the bin was not emptied.

Crossing back to the west side of Nelson Road, Mr Giltrow headed for The Cottage perched on the higher ground away from the roadside. Towards the end of its days (in the 1960s) a man named Basel-White owned this 'honest sized house' when it was known as Retreat Cottage and where he bred Airedales.

In 1901, the head of the household was away on Census Night, leaving boarder, 19-year-old farm labourer John Horne from Kent alone with 18-year-old domestic cook Olive Hill and 17-year-old domestic housemaid Florence Fance. This risqué situation may well have set tongues wagging in the Red Lion public House on the opposite side of Nelson Road, glimpsed below as the building immediately behind the telegraph pole. The Market Place and what is now The Triangle Café (left) were six years away from Mr Giltrow's enumeration.

The Red Lion was the second of Whitton's drinking houses, built in 1819 and the only one subsequently lost to developers. Jesse Baker was landlord in 1901, having moved to Whitton nine months previously when his daughter, Fanny, was born. With his wife, Sarah, was 12-year-old niece, Noble. By the 1930s The Red Lion had ceased trading as a public house. One of its back rooms was used as Whitton's first bank before The Midland built its branch in the High Street next to the new station. The rest of the building was used by a coal merchant called Bernhardt whose two burly daughters helped keep the home fires burning during World War Two by lugging 100 weight sacks of coal around Whitton.

Apart from the Postman's Rest Cottages, The Red Lion stood as the only built structure on the east side of Nelson Road until 1906. It was demolished sometime after the Second World War and Numbers 57-75 Nelson Road now occupy the site.

Re-crossing to the west side of Nelson Road, Mr Giltrow called on Elm Cottage, which like its neighbour, The Cottage, stood detached in its owns grounds but was much smaller and built closer to the roadside. It was occupied by Georgina Ferguson, a 55-year-old widow living on her own means. Sharing the four rooms was her son, Frederick, a 23-year-old sergeant in the army who was born in Surrey.

Susan Hewitt living next door in 1, Pope's Cottages was a domestic working from home. Living with her was her son and daughter, 21-year-old Albert, a general labourer, and 16-year-old Clara. In 1881, then aged 44, Susan Hewitt was living in the same cottage with her labourer husband, Richard, also from Oxfordshire. The eldest child at home then was Rosette who was born in Whitton in 1872. Her brother Alfred arrived two years later, followed by Albert, who was then aged one. Two fellow labourers, Henry Atkins and Thomas Collier completed the household as lodgers. In 1891 all the children were accounted for, but 52-year-old Emma from Isleworth had replaced Susan as Richard Hewitt's wife, yet Susan re-appears as a widow in Mr Giltrow's enumeration a decade later.

Pope's Cottages suffered huge problems with drains, compounded by their situation on the lower ground at the roadside and their close proximity to two piggeries. The byelaw requiring swine to be kept no closer than 100 yards from dwelling houses was commonly disregarded, constituting a nuisance or an injury to public health. Although the sties behind Pope's Cottages had asphalted floors there was no drainage save for that which flowed along a trench into an adjacent garden, which was full of fetid fluid. The rest flowed into a ditch that discharged into a neighbouring stream. Eventually the condition was recognised as a 'severe danger to occupiers' by reason of contamination to the low wells from where they obtained their drinking water, grossly polluted with much 'oxidised organic matter' and 'quite unfit for dietetic use'.

Then there was the smell, especially in summer, added to which was a lack of manure pits to manage the slop refuse. Provision for human waste was no better. The privies were of the 'old type', badly constructed and unhygienic. Market garden labourer George Neale had been living in these conditions in number one Pope's Cottages (pictured left below) before 1890 when his son, also called George, was born. Four years later and he was still in residence with his wife, Sarah and a second son, Ernest, and two year old daughter, May.

The Village, Whitton.   W.H.A. 2542.

In number three Mr Giltrow recorded Sarah Rogers, a 54-year-old widowed gardener's labourer. Her daughter Henrietta was a domestic servant and her 16-year-old son, Henry, an agricultural labourer. Charles Flippance, also an agricultural labourer, who headed the household of number four, came to Whitton from Kent before 1893 when his son Charles was born. One of the cottage's three habitable rooms was let to Mary Cooley, a 66-year-old widow from Devizes who Mr Giltrow recorded as blind. Occupying number five Pope's Cottages were bricklayer's labourer John Nash, his wife Lavinia and their 13-year-old son, George. Both Lavinia and George were born in Worcester, indicating that John had been living and working there until returning to his native Twickenham. Pope's Cottages were demolished in the 1960s to make way for the new housing we see today.

What John Burridge Giltrow recorded as Parec Cottage and his predecessor a decade earlier listed simply as 'Grocers Shop' (now replaced with 24 Nelson Road) shared a similar fate. This was the long, thin retail premises pictured opposite declaring the sign 'Batey'. Measuring just 14 feet wide, it was previously occupied by a series of agricultural labouring families until Mr Giltrow recorded 70-year-old George Parris from Stepney running a Printers and Stationary business there with his sister, Emma, who was born south of the Thames in Lambeth. Five or six years after Mr Giltrow's enumeration, the premises would become one of three teashops in the village catering for the cycling craze, with Whitton a popular halt for Londoners on a day out in the country. It would also court notoriety when one owner was variously accused of murdering a vagrant on Twickenham Green and swindling an elderly woman of her life savings before murdering her too. The case was dismissed due to conflicting evidence and the accused fled to Ireland.

The somewhat forlorn, detached house (below, centre) languishing today as 8, Nelson Road was entered in the 1891 census as Murray's Cottage, when it consisted of five separate households. Mr Giltrow records half the same building as Murray's Cottage and the other as The Statue.

With deeds dating back to the 16th century, what survives clad in its stuccoed overcoat and its symmetrical composition is Whitton's sole example of architecture influenced by the Georgian period. John Plaw in his Sketches for Country Houses, *Villas and Rural Dwellings* (1800) features exactly this style of classical residence, described as 'a very comfortable residence for a family with a small independent fortune, or a retreat [in which] occasionally to relax from the bustle of business'.

The bricked up centre window over the front door recalls the Window Tax, which like the Hearth Tax before it was imposed on domestic dwellings under the Act of 1662 to reorganise the revenues of the crown following the Restoration. The interior still retains four rooms downstairs in the classic Georgian fashion. From the front door off a central hallway was the common parlour measuring 12 feet by 13 feet. Opposite was a smaller study 10 feet by 12 feet to accommodate the flight of stairs. To the back was a kitchen and back parlour, each measuring 12 by 13 feet. Often a washhouse and bakehouse attached either side of the building, whereas they are to the rear in this example.

Where a conservatory measuring in the region of nine feet by sixteen feet often attached the other side, a rear access to the lower quarters at the north end and an open stairwell to the upper rooms at the south maintain the balance. Upstairs are two bedrooms at the back each measuring 12 feet by 13 feet, and two to the front each measuring 10 feet by 12 feet leading off a small landing area of about six by twelve feet once lit by the central window before it was bricked up.

The interior underwent exhaustive and unfortunate alteration in the 1940s. Further 'improvements' in 1998 introduced entirely unsympathetic white PVC windows and matching front door replacing one of solid wood, which boasted a small diamond shaped window below the legend made out in gold lettering: 'The Statue'. Why it took this name is not known. Its previous incarnation as Murray's Cottage took the name of the chief landowner, as did other properties throughout Whitton. Speculation has it that in its design and layout, including its expansive yard and stabling, the building was originally an Inn called The Statue sometime in its long history.

The exterior stairwell possibly offering access to overnight accommodation avoiding the bar area downstairs is the only evidence to suggest this. Today the building provides for multi-occupancy just as it did at the time of Mr Giltrow's enumeration. Then it was split between two households. R W Swaker, a local councillor, occupied the lower half known as The Statue. As a developer he would go on to have a profound impact on the built Whitton landscape. Born in Watford in 1851, R W Swaker moved with his family to Hampshire five years later where his sister, entered in Mr Giltrow's schedule simply as 'C' Swaker was born. R W was married sometime before 1878 when his eldest child, a daughter recorded as 'S. E' was born in Kidderminster. Her younger sister, 'E.C' was born in Acton in 1890 and four years later the family had moved to Chiswick where R.W's youngest son 'W.C.' was born. Sometime after 1897 the family moved to Whitton.

In 1901, R W is recorded as married and not a widower, but with no mention of a wife. His sister, 'C', was employed as cook and Robert, the eldest boy and the only member of the family to be afforded a name beyond that of an initial, was boarding in the upper half of the building still recorded as Murray's Cottage. Here Walter Baker was head of the household, having moved from Richmond with his wife, Mary and their three children. From an Agreement dated 10th May 1869 between Mr & Mrs William James Baker of Paved Court, Richmond, and others with Mr Silas Paul Baker, we can reasonably assume that Walter Baker was a relation.

The Agreement was part of an extensive title search by the Strand firm of solicitors Chinery & Aldridge, which took a full year to complete from January 1869. As well as the 'copyhold cottage with garden and land', the estate included two other properties close by. Formerly the copyhold estate of Edward Bird of Twickenham, Bird's son, also called Edward, died intestate and a bachelor, leaving as coheiresses his two sisters, one of whom, Sarah, was admitted to the estate with her husband Henry Baker, their children, their heirs and assigns 'for ever as tenants in common'. In 1881 Silas Baker is recorded as a timber merchant, which might account for the long, thin building attaching the yard as a site office or a store for cut timber. Ten years earlier he was in the asphalt supply business.

Oil-based asphalt from Trinidad was by this time used to lay on top of reinforced concrete road surfaces, although most roads continued to be maintained by local authorities more interested in doing the least work at the most profit. Typically, Whitton's main thoroughfares were made up of thousands of Jarrah wood paving blocks, which were pitched in tar in an 80-gallon mobile boiler as they were laid. In extreme weather these blocks tended to expand and in turn rise up and become loose. Although unpopular with road users, they did burn well and provided a useful, if illicit, supply of winter fuel.

On Census Night, 1901, Walter Baker declared his occupation to be that of a sewer pipe drainer. R W Swaker declared himself to be a building contractor. Nineteen days later, the Highways and Fire Brigade Committee were considering tenders for new soil and surface water sewers along Kneller Road and Hounslow Road. Recommend for the work was R W Swaker at £1,015.15s.0d. His tender duly accepted work was in hand two months later. The Statue had by then effectively become the headquarters of Whitton's advance into the realms of 20th century sanitation.

The Twickenham Local Board had been applying pressure on the Grand Junction Water Works Company since 1893 to provide a better water supply to Whitton. The Metropolis Water Act of 1852 prohibited the taking of water from the tidal Thames, which meant that water had to be taken from above Teddington Lock. In practical terms the first suitable location with land available for Waterworks was Hampton. As a consequence, the Southwark and Vauxhall, the Grand Junction and the West Middlesex Water Companies all established works there. Only parts of Whitton enjoyed a piped water supply. By 1900 the old pumps at the Nelson Road end of Hospital Bridge Road serving the district had become defective and were reported to be in a 'tumble down state, requiring a complete overhaul'. Rainwater collected in tubs and underground wells were in common use in Whitton deep into the 20th century.

What are today numbers 6, 4 and 2, Nelson Road were recorded in 1901 as White Hart Cottages and are contemporaneous in date with the four cottages adjoining The White Hart around the corner in Kneller Road. John Smith, a soldier in the 2nd Lincolnshire Regiment was the Head of the household in the cottage neighbouring The Statue. His wife, Sarah, was born in Surrey and three of their four children aged from five years to 11 months were born in Whitton. Sixty-six year old Mary Allen lived next door with boarders, probably relatives, Alfred Allen, a public house potman, and Walter Allen, a gardener's labourer. And in the end cottage Mr Giltrow recorded George Warren, a 50 year old general labourer from Essex, his daughter, Clara, who was working at home as housekeeper, and son Henry, a butcher's assistant. Like most all of the dwellings hereabouts, these were at one time condemned by the Medical Officer for Health as unfit for human habitation, but managed to survive demolition first in 1914, and again in the 1960s.

Hereafter, the exact perambulations of Whitton's enumerators becomes confused. Having at this point returned a complete circumnavigation of all Whitton households, Mr Giltrow's immediate predecessor scheduled Austen Cottage, where agricultural labourers Thomas and Mary Hamilton were living and where their son, George, was born. The whereabouts of Austen Cottage presents something of a mystery until we follow Mr Giltrow's route back to his home in High Street Hounslow to include two stragglers.

The first was student bandsman Richard Banbury, his wife Susan and their four-year-old daughter, Gertrude, who were billeted at the Married Quarters, Kneller Hall. The second was the irascible occupant of number eight Whitton Park Terrace who had earlier showered Mr Giltrow with abuse. To reach him from The Married Quarters, Mr Giltrow could have taken Kneller Road to Hounslow Road and turned right en route for home. Or he could have turned into Whitton Dean to arrive at much the same point. Had he done so then he would have passed by another of the Lodges dotted around the circumference of the former estate.

Prior to its demolition in the 1960s, Dean Lodge stood opposite the Drill Ground (now Murray Park) just inside the borough of Heston and Isleworth. But given the tenuous nature of the parish boundaries along Whitton Dean, it is highly likely that it was included in the 1891 census as Austen Cottage and by Mr Giltrow as 'Whitton Park Estate'.

As this photograph taken in the 1960s shows, the building was semi-detached and in keeping with the style of the surviving lodges on Nelson Road. Having secured the details of John Philpot, an Essex born railway platelayer and his family, John Burridge Giltrow made his way west along Whitton Dean to knock again on the door of 8, Whitton Park Terrace where he identified his former abuser as 61-year-old Thomas Watts, a commission agent born in Bury St Edmunds and his wife, Eliza, late of that same parish. Thus the physical part of Mr Giltrow's enumeration was at an end. His predecessor in 1891, however, finished on a more sombre note, happening as he did across 68 year old John Brown, an agricultural labourer from Isleworth, whose poignant declaration in the census of that year reads 'No House.'

CULMINATION AND CONCLUSIONS

Sunday 8th April 1901 was the last opportunity for John Burridge Giltrow to pick up on stragglers. Back home in the house or rooms he shared with his wife, Alice, in Hounslow Town, he sorted the final details and copied them 'very legibly in ink' into his Censor Enumerator's Book. First, in the spaces at the top of the page, was entered the name of the appropriate Civil Parish, Ecclesiastical Parish, County or Municipal Borough or Urban District, Ward, Rural District, Parliamentary Borough or Division, Town, Village or Hamlet.

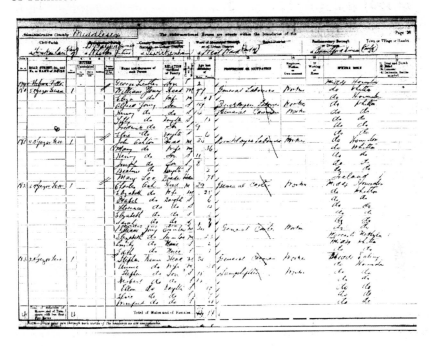

The first column numbered each individual schedule. In the second was entered the road or street name, or where the house was situated, the number of the house and any distinctive name by which it was known. The third column indicated an inhabited or uninhabited house. Where there were two or more occupiers in the same house, double lines were drawn to distinguish the separate households. Even a single person living alone was treated as a separate household and recorded as the head accordingly.

No abbreviations were allowed except those authorised, such as 'daur' for daughter, 'M in law' for Mother in law, 'Serv' for servant, and so on. First Christian names were written in full, adding the initials of other names where appropriate. 'Do' (ditto) was used where the same surname occurred in succession. At the foot of each page the total number of Schedules was added, plus the number of houses, tenements of less than 5 rooms and the numbers of males and females.

Having carefully checked all of the returned schedules and doing his utmost to ensure that there were no obvious gaps or inconsistencies, John Burridge Giltrow signed off his enumeration on Sunday 15th April 1901 and submitted his declaration to the Registrar, Ellen B Stickley, on the occasion of her third examination of Whitton's habitation since the census of 1881.

Following her own scrutiny of the particulars contained in Mr Giltrow's CEB, Ellen Stickley duly signed off the Return four days later, which was witnessed by the Superintendent Registrar on 26th April. At the Census Office in London, a small army of clerks checked the data for accuracy before extracting specific categories of information. This was in turn compiled into tables and used in the Census Report, which recorded the whole of the population of England and Wales on 1 April 1901.

In 1881, the population of Whitton stood at 712, of which just over 9%, or 66, were military personnel and their families. In 1891, of the 769 inhabitants of Whitton, 65, or around 8.5% were married soldiers and their families billeted in the village. By 1891 the population had risen to 955. The Married Quarters attaching Kneller Hall had been built, housing the same number of married students and their families (66), plus two more occupying the Lodges. With the military element out of the equation, the civilian population had increased by just over 100. The Report for Twickenham showed an increase in overall population of 5,695 since 1891, which was at variance with the council's understanding of its rateable demographics. In assuming that one in every five persons was entitled to be a parochial elector, it was decided that the Council would be better able to judge or form an opinion as to the accuracy of the count after a rate return was prepared.

However, 'through the kindness of the Rev. H P Prosser,' the Town Clerk was able to confirm the Ecclesiastical Parishes agreed with the Census, showing a total population of 20,991, with St Mary 6,068, Holy Trinity 7,996, St Stephen 5,809 and St Philip & St James (Whitton), including all military service personnel attached to Kneller Hall, 1,118.

Although the market gardening industry in Middlesex (including London) was continuing its gravitation to Kent, agricultural labourers remained the largest sector of Whitton's working population. Oxfordshire looms large as the most consistent source of seasonal labour and eventual settlement, followed by Buckinghamshire. Those arriving from London mostly came from the former market garden districts of Kensington and Chelsea.

Measures to improve the living conditions of the poorest were in place, although it would be years before they would have any lasting effect. The several Bills dealing with the powers and duties of local authorities were being used, for example the imposition of penalties for the supply of impure or unwholesome water for domestic use. Owners of property declared to be unhealthy would soon be compelled to clear the sites at their own cost, and the creation of a 'Fair Rent Court' could result in a rent reduction where considered appropriate.

Twickenham Local Board had been considering the question of The Housing of the Working Classes Act since it was passed through Parliament in 1890. A Committee set up in 1900 had yet to 'ascertain whether there had been formed or there was 'in the course of formation within their districts any area or areas to which persons of vicious, degraded or immoral habits resort as temporary or permanent residents in lodging-houses or other tenements'. Although some measures had been brought about, 'much evils' still remained to be remedied. Inquiry followed inquiry, during which time the shortage of decent housing accommodation in Whitton was exacerbated with the loss due to demolition of at least 12 units. A World War later and the first houses built specifically for the working classes appeared in Whitton. Post Thatcher and the right to buy, that provision has gone, leaving the local authority now looking to partnerships in the creation of 'affordable housing' for 'key workers'.

Apart two recorded incidents of crippling illness during Mr Giltrow's enumeration; one positive deficiency was identified in the apparent lack of unemployment. The census of 1881 recorded half a dozen unemployed men in Whitton. In 1891 there were none. Most of those unemployed in 1881 were not involved in agriculture or horti-culture. Lady Day (25th March), a week or so before the census was taken, was still common parlance in 1901. It marked to country folk since medieval times the start of the New Year when work began in earnest after the winter lull. The soil was soft enough for plough teams to turn over the first fallow fields and preparations could begin for the sowing of spring crops of barley, oats, peas and beans.

Thereafter, the full range of Whitton's agricultural and horticultur-al activities geared up into summer and autumn until the third and final ploughing took place prior to the sowing of winter crops of wheat and rye and the planting of spring bulbs. Martinmas (11 November) was the traditional day for slaughtering and salting of old stock and swine and where little of Whitton's copious pig pop-ulation was wasted. The flesh provided meat and the skin could be cured into tough leather.

By mid-November, Whitton's agrarian workforce prepared for the lean times ahead. Unlike their medieval forebears, there were no wild woods to collect fuel for the fire, or peat to cut. Money had to be found to provide for coal. With almost all the outdoor work complete in the fields, the women would continue earning money cleaning, washing, ironing and other domestic work, but fewer men would be required caring for the animals, general farm maintenance and ploughing beyond December.

It would be reasonable to assume that many looked to casual labour-ing jobs, although the borough Surveyor's report of 6 September 1900 suggests otherwise, bemoaning the work proceeding slowly on the new sewers being dug in Kneller Road and Hounslow Road, due to a lack of local labour. The first formal definition of unemploy-ment was incorporated into the popular vocabulary of social reform after 1895 when it became the concern of politicians and leaders of the organised working class. Policies emerged aimed at providing artificial relief works, thereby eliminating unemployment.

The firms of Messrs J Mowlem & Co., and Messrs G Wimpey & Co., were the biggest employers of local casual labourers locally, with as many as 100 men on their books at any one time. A Labour Bureau opened at the council depot in King Street, Twickenham three years after Mr Giltrow's Enumeration where unemployed local workmen could register their names to earn three shillings for an eight-hour day either levelling or digging the gravel pits in Hospital Bridge Road and Whitton Dean. Within a year 168 men had taken up this employment or other causal work such as sweeping or scavenging.

Mr Giltrow's enumeration took place at a particular moment in time with regard to Whitton's historical and social record. The rapid growth of the Capital at the turn of the last century ignited a smouldering ember first lit in Whitton by Louis Kyezor in the 1840s. Then his restraints on anti-social behaviour revived the fortunes of an ailing rural village, which, coupled with the restored power and influence of Whitton Park, created a classic Victorian societal model. Fifty years later and it was for sale. By the census of 1911, the first expansion of Old Whitton's medieval street plan was complete.

195

Between 1903 and 1910 speculative builders including R W Swaker had altered the landscape forever with the cutting of Colonial Avenue (above) and Cedar Avenue. Other new houses were going up along Kneller Road, Nelson Road, Percy Road and on the fringes of Whitton Park. Seaton Road was begun in 1905 with 16 terraced houses facing Frank Peacock's piggery. By the census of 1921 the local authority had begun to fill in the holes left by the developers with housing in Kneller Road, Colonial Avenue, Cedar Avenue and in the ultimate creation of Prospect Crescent.

After direct access to Whitton by rail by 1931 came the new Chertsey Arterial (A316), which not only offered another escape route from the slums and overcrowding of the Capital, but also for the first time in history halted the need to travel via Richmond or Brentford to reach Whitton. With this direct access came the wholesale development synonymous with the inter-war years. Drawing an imaginary line south of Nelson Road and Warren Road, nothing exists on the built landscape older than 1935 other than two cemeteries and some Victorian building towards Hospital Bridge Road.

196

Fields familiar to John Burridge Giltrow are now neatly packaged into thousands of individual parcels fronting and flanking multiple examples of the suburban ideal. Only Heathfield Recreation ground towards Bridge Farm offers a hint of the landscape before urbanisation when fewer than 10% of households in the London area were owner-occupiers with local authority and philanthropic housing accounting for less than 5%. Nearly 90% rented privately.

The First World War accentuated an already growing housing crisis making it less desirable to be a landlord. Inflation made it too expensive for private house builders to build new homes at a worthwhile rentable value. With no new house building, the resulting shortage saw landlords attempt to exploit the scarcity of the market by raising rents, which resulted in the government introducing rent control. The Depression of the 1930s saw existing homeowners defaulting on their mortgages. But while rates of homeownership fell and with conditions depressed elsewhere, London enjoyed a boom period for the growth of home ownership.

Most Londoners still had jobs and when prices and interest rates fell dramatically, money with which to buy a house became very cheap to borrow. With so little new industrial development taking place, building societies especially found they had a huge amount of money to lend. Although they had been in existence for over a century, in business mostly to lend money to builders and landlords, in the 1920s and 1930s they started to direct their attention towards potential owner-occupiers. Likewise, civil engineering companies such as Wates and Wimpey, who switched to the mass production of housing, with the emphasis not just on homes but on the fresh concept of lifestyle.

Unlike the very rich, it was important for the lower middle classes to possess their own piece of land. In this, their expansion became more and more important as a factor stimulating the growth of home ownership in the middle decades of the 20th century. The population of Whitton in 1930 stood at 4,000. In less than five years that number had increased ten fold. The people who came to settle were a new breed of the better off incomers who began to arrive after the 1840s when the village began to expand.

Then, the large houses occupied by the relatively wealthy were regarded as provincial. All else were country folk. A century later and Whitton was transformed into what historians, sociologists and pundits have defined as a suburb.

In Shakespeare's London many houses of prostitution were found on the outskirts of the city where whores were known as 'suburb sinners'. To call a man a 'suburbanite' then was a serious insult. Chaucer has the impious Canon's Yeoman and his master, a crooked alchemist living in 'in the suburbes of town', lurking in corners and blind alleys 'where robbers and thieves instinctively huddle secretly and fearfully together'.

Whitton's historical legacy is built on the principle that Twickenham and Richmond traditionally represented the appropriate setting for the elite. After the 18th century, Whitton sat as a largely disreputable zone to which the poorest inhabitants were attracted. The social distinctions are enshrined in the language used by antiquarians, historians and local government. Social reformer Louis Kyezor described a place of 'inferior, debased, licentious order', whereas today of all of the 'villages' comprising the London Borough of Richmond upon Thames, Whitton is the safest and most crime-free.

Where Whitton fails in the definition of a suburb is as an area predominantly inhabited by the middle classes to the exclusion of industry and lower-class residents. Similarly the aesthetic 'marriage of town and country' taken to be the mark of the true suburb. Although thousands of Whitton inhabitants depend economically on jobs in London, it is not dependent on the Capital for many of the major institutions of urban life such as professional services, department stores and other specialized shops, hospitals and culture. For what it lacks in those areas, there are the neighbouring towns of Richmond, Twickenham and Hounslow, themselves perceived suburbs of the capital.

The definition of community better suits Whitton; where a specific group of people living in a defined geographical area largely subscribe to a common culture, share values and norms arranged in a social structure according to relationships that have developed over a period of time. But that period of time is as brief as it is recent. People are said to be born into a community and choose to live in a suburb. Before 1901 more people chose to live in Whitton. That factor was reversed after 1931 and a community maintained for more than a century after Mr Giltrow's enumeration.

SOURCES & FURTHER READING

Primary Sources

1. Archival
<u>Metropolitan Archive</u>
Report on the deeds of the Whitton Park Estate, Twickenham 1621-1824. Accession 1149.
Report on the Bridges of Middlesex. 1825.
Tithe Redemption. 1846.
<u>Richmond upon Thames Local Studies Collection</u>
Twickenham Local Board Minutes 1891 – 1895
Twickenham Urban District Council Minutes 1895 - 1930
Census Returns 1881, 1891, 1901
Richmond Times Directory Almanac 1891
Richmond & Twickenham Times Almanac 1881 / 1888
Directories for Twickenham and Whitton 1860 –1882
Kelly's Middlesex Directory 1882
Kelly's Directory of Richmond, Kew etc. 1902/3 / 1907
Twickenham Rate Book 1895
Auction catalogue: Kneller Hall Estate. 1841
Whitton Park Estate sales catalogues 1894- 1910
The Book of Twickenham.
Health Board Records / Medical Officer of Health

2. Newspapers & Periodicals
<u>Richmond upon Thames Local Studies Collection</u>
Middlesex Chronicle
Richmond & Twickenham Times
Thames Valley Times
Richmond Herald

3. Maps
<u>Richmond upon Thames Local Studies Collection</u>
Ordnance Survey: Northern Twickenham and Whitton 6-inch. 1867
Ordnance Survey 15 inch. 1894-6
Ordnance Survey 6 inch. Re-levelled 1913
Ordnance Survey 25 inch. 1960

3. Maps (cont.)
Plan of the Parish of Twickenham 1846
Treswell, Ralph. 1607. Syon MSS B XIII 2a
Glover, Moses. 1635. Syon MSS B XIII
Rocque, John. 1741-5
Sauthier. C.J. 1786/7. Syon MSS XIII 2e
Ordnance Surveryors' Drawings of the London Area 1799-1808.
OSD.27/Serial No.83. Hampton Court 1804-6 (2" to mile)
Cary's Actual Survey of the County Ten Miles round Hampton Court and Richmond
Milne, Thomas. Land Use Map. 1800. (British Museum KTOP VI (95) – reprinted with commentary by the London Topographical Society. 1975).
Twickenham Enclosure Award. 1813. Middlesex Record Office
Isleworth and Heston Enclosure Award. 1813. Hounslow Local Studies.
Plan of Kneller Hall Estate situate at Whitton. 1841
Twickenham Copyholds in the Paris of Isleworth. 1842.
Warren. W.T. Plan of the Parish Twickenham 1813 /14 /45/ 46 /50.

4. Oral Accounts
Carverhill, Mrs. (1995) Whitton 1915 -1995
Costa E (1990) Whitton 1895 - 1995
Duran J (1995) Whitton 1900 - 1995
King G (1992) Hounslow / Whitton 1930 - 1997
Tulip D (1993) Whitton 1925 -
Underwood H (1992) Whitton 1901- 1992

Secondary Sources
Borough of Twickenham Local History Society Papers:
Foster, P and Simpson D.H. Whitton Park and Whitton Place. Paper No.41. 1979
Urwin, A C B. Commercial Nurseries and Market Gardens. Borough of Twickenham History Society Paper no 50. 1982 .
Urwin, A C B. Birket's Brook. Borough of Twickenham History Society. 1971
A.C.B. Urwin. A C B. (1978) Twickenham and Whitton. Some Evidence of Early Land Development: 1214 to 1644. Borough of Twickenham Local History Society. Paper 40.

Secondary Sources (cont.)

Borough of Twickenham Local History Society Papers:Cashmore, T H R.
Richard Cobbett's Twickenham - 1866-1872, Borough of Twickenham
Local History Society Paper No53, 1984, p27

Cashmore, T H R. Twickenham in 1818, the Year of the Enclosure,
Borough of Twickenham Local history Society Paper No38, 1977

Urwin, A C B. The Coming of Electricity to Twickenham. BoTLHS Paper
37. 1977

Barnfield, P D. Protestant Nonconformity in Twickenham, Whitton,
Teddington and The Hamptons. Paper 59. 1987.

Pearce, Brian Louis. The Fashioned Reed. Paper no 67. 1992.

Pearce, B L. Free For All: The Public Library Movement in Twickenham.
Paper No.55. 1985.

Cashmore, T H R. The Mystery of Thomas Haydon Green. The Whitton
Murder and the Cato Street Conspiracy. Paper No. 23. 1972.

Members of BoTLHS. One hundred years of shopping in the old borough of Twickenham. Paper No.79. 1999.

Pollins, Harold and Rosewarne, Vic. Louis Kyezor The King of Whitton
c1796 –1869. Paper No. 82. 2002.

Borough of Twickenham Local History Society. Twickenham as it was.
1976.

Borough of Twickenham Local History Society. Bygone
Twickenham.1983.

Hounslow & District History Society. Hounslow as it was. 1987.

Cherry, M, Howe, K, Sheaf, J. Britain in old photographs. Twickenham,
Teddington & Hampton. 1998.

Further Reading

Bate. G.E. And So Make a City Here: The Story of a Lost Heathland.
Thomasons Ltd. 1948.

Bennett, L.G. The Horticultural History of Middlesex. 1952

Brewer. History of Middlesex. 1816.

Buchan. S. Water Supply of the County of London. 1938

Cobbett. R.S. Memorials of Twickenham. 1872

Daunton, M J. Royal Mail: The Post Office since 1840. Athlone
Press.1985.

Day, M.J. Horticultural History of SW Middlesex (BA dissertation.
Durham University) 1964

Further Reading (cont.)

Donnachie.I. Landscapes, buildings and physical artefacts. Sources and Methods: A Handbook. Michael Drake and Ruth Finnegan (Eds). The Open University. 1997

Drake, M and Finnegan (Ed). Studying Family and Community History. Vol4. Sources and Methods. Open University. 1997

Hardcastle, H C. Whitton: A Village Within A Suburb. 1987

Harvey, John. Nurseries in Milne's Land Use Map. (London and Middlesex Archeological Society) 1973.

Kitson, G. The Making of Victorian England Methuen, 1962. p 122

Marwick, Arthur. Primary Sources (Chapter 2) Sources and Methods: A Handbook. Michael Drake and Ruth Finnegan (Eds). The Open University. 1992.

Maxwell, Gordon. S. Highwayman's Heath. Thomasons Ltd. (first pub.1935, 1938. New Edition (re-set) 1949.

Page, William (Ed). A History of the County of Middlesex: Volume II. 1911.

Perry, George. The Great British Picture Show. Paladin. 1975

Simpson, Donald (Ed). Twickenham Past. Historical Publications, 1993

Stannard, Colin. London Bus Magazine: Golden Jubilee Celebrations (1933-53). London Transport publications. 1953.

Turner, Gordon and Turner, Alwyn W. The Trumpets Will Sound: The Story of the Royal Military School of Music Kneller Hall. Papares Ltd. 1996.

Vulliamy, C E. Archaeology of Middlesex

Whitehand, JWR and Carr. Christine M.H. Morphological periods, planning and reality: the case of England's inter-war suburbs. Urban History, 26, 2.1999.

Williams M A. Researching Local History. London: Longman. 1996.

Wolfston, Patricia S. Revised by Clifford Webb. Greater London Cemeteries and Crematoria. Society of Genealogists.

ACKNOWLEDGEMENTS

My thanks and appreciation in particular to Dr Chris French and all those associated with the Kingston University Masters Degree in Local History, to Jane Baxter and staff at the Richmond upon Thames Local Studies Collection for their unstinting help and assistance throughout the research process. Also to the many members of the Borough of Twickenham Local History Society past and present for the rich historical legacy they have provided in written Papers, and to those local residents of Whitton who kindly gave of their time to share their memories, documents and photographs.

INDEX

A316 Great Chertsey Road, 146
Admiral (or Lord) Nelson
  The, 102
Albert Cottage, 93
Albert Villa, 93, 94
Alden
  Ann, 156
Alder
  Frederick, 173
Aldridge
  Charles, 49
Alexander
  James, 141
Allen
Alfred, 188
  Frank, 28
  Mary, 188
  Walter, 188
Allenson
  Elizabeth, 39, 40, 41, 172
  James, 39
Alma Cottages, 108
Alma Villas, 111
Alton Cottage, 21
Alton Gardens, 19
Alton Villa, 21, 22
Anderson
  Helen, 99
  Jane and Elizabeth, 98, 102
  Old Rob, 99
Anderson Cottages, 164
Andrews
  William, 130
Andrews Farm, 128
Anstead
  Frank, 152
Applethorpe Lodge, 156
Archdeacon Cambridge School, 33
Arlotte
  Manfred, 21
Ash
  Charles, 168
Ashton
  John, 168

Joseph, 170
  Sarah, 170
Aspray
  Charles, 59, 60
Atkin
  Francis, 170
Atkins
  Henry, 182
Auderon
  Alice, 96
Aussand
  Henry, 131
Austen Cottage, 188
Ayliff
  Charles, 45

Backland
  Matilda, 175
Bacon
  Jamie, 157
Baker
  George, 179
  Henry, 186
  Jesse, 181
  Silas Paul, 186
  Walter, 186
  William James, 186
Balchin
  John, 131
Balls
  Maurice, 113
Barker
  Charles, 118
Barrington-Foote
  Colonel, 20
Barton
  George, 89
Beebohn Tree
  Sir Henry, 60
Beerhouse Act, 27
Belasyse
  Baron John, 24, 112
Bell Road, 15, 18

Benn
  Stephen, 168
Bennett
  Ada, 153
  George, 152
Benns Cottage, 118
Bicknell
  William, 104
Biggens
  Charles, 111
Bird
  Edward, 186
Birket's Brook, 11, 36, 200
Bishop
  W, 179
Bishop Perrin Memorial Church of
  England School, 143
Boxall
  George, 131
Bradley
  Thomas, 153
  William, 92, 153
Brennan
  John, 156
Brett
  Sir Robert, 147
Bricknell
  Henry, 131
Bridge Farm Nursery, 138
Bridge Way, 179
Brister
  Samuel, 158
Brown
  Alfred, 110
Bessie, 123
  James, 164
  Jesse, 49, 59
  John, 119, 130, 189
  Lydia, 163
  Richard, 154
  William, 130
Browning
  Albert, 124
Burr
  Edith, 117
Butler

John, 46
Leopold, 156

Cailes
  Henry, 118
Camellia Close, 115
Campbell
    Archibald. See Lord Islay
    Archibald, Lord Ilay, 67
Carol
    Clara, 115
Carr
    Elizabeth, 114
    Sergeant, 29, 202
Carrington Avenue, 76
  Carter
    Frederick, 84
    John, 114
Cato Street Conspiracy, 87, 201
Cedar Avenue, 195
Cedars
    The, 113
Cemetery Lodge, 126, 142
Chadwick
    Edwin, 43
Chance
    Richard, 28
Chapman
    Henry, 111
Chase Bridge, 6, 11, 12, 14, 17, 18,
    19, 21, 25
Chase,
    William, 11, 25
Cherrett
    Elizabeth, 26
Chertsey Road, 5, 24, 146, 171
Clarence Terrace, 38, 39
Clark
    Edmund, 109
Clarke
    Capt. John, 115
    Decimus, 6, 21, 22, 121
    Jane, 123
    Mary, 106
    William, 123

Clement
  Elizabeth, 126
  James, 126
  Lavinia, 126
  Mary, 180
Clifford
  William, 111
Cobbett
  Rev. R S, 179
  William, 144
Cole
  Richard, 115
Coleopy
  Flora, 98
Coles
  Charles, 122
  Frederick, 128
Coles Bridge, 18
Collier
  Thomas, 182
Collingwood Close, 118
Collins
  Henry, 110
Colonial Avenue, 2, 52, 55, 83, 195
Colonial Villas, 83
Constable
  Robert, 24
Constance Road, 114, 150
Conway Road, 124
Cooke
  Edmund, 22
Cooley
  Mary, 183
Coombs
  Frederick, 45
Cooper, 77, 78, 84, 96, 102
  Charles & Mabel, 77
  Marion, 84
Corrington
  Jesse, 170
Coster
  Ted, 83
Cottage Hospital, 59
Cottle
  George, 126
Cox

George, 88
  Samuel, 45
Crane Park Nature Reserve, 132
Croft
  The, 30, 31, 32, 175
Cullerne
  Robert, 115
Curtis and Harvey, 129
Cushing
  Thomas, 82
Cutt
  Alfred, 163

Daisy Cottages, 150
Dalrymple
  Lady Laura, 130
Darnford
  Arthur, 131
Davison
  George, 172
Dean
  Arthur, 37, 54, 93
Dean Lodge, 188
Donaghue
  David, 173
Donaldson
  Amy, 80
Drewett
  Sarah, 89
Drill Hall, 54, 55
Duke of Cambridge public house, 25
Duke of Northumberland's River,
  11, 12, 18
Duke of York
  Public House, 138
Dunn
  Frederick, 109
Dysart
  Countess, 130

Eastland
  James, 73
Eden

Ann, 160
Edith Cottages, 48
Edward
    Hannah, 28, 53, 55, 56, 72, 97
Edwards
    George, 87. See Thomas Haydon
    Green
Edy
    George, 44
Elden
    William, 96
Elliott
    John, 128
Elm Cottage, 182
Elmes
    Harriet, 154
Elms
    John, 154
Elsley
    William, 102
Emma's Cottage, 25
Emmanuel
    Eliza, 26
    Morris, 24, 26, 79
Escott
    William, 96
Evan
    James, 83
Evelyn Close, 117

Fairlight, 115
Fairmead Estate, 54
Fance
    Florence, 181
Farmer
    Henry, 131
    Thomas, 157
Faulkner
    William and Harriet, 29
Feltham Curve
    The, 117
Feltham Marshalling Yards, 125
Fenwick
    Thomas Wright, 59
Ferguson

Georgina, 182
Field
    Arthur, 142
    Frederick, 141
Field's Garage, 47
Fiestler
    Carl, 165
Firman
    Ellen, 73
Fisher
    Arthur, 161
Fitzwalter
    William, 153
Flippance
    Charles, 183
Forge
    The, 47, 48, 49, 180
Francis
    Edwin, 28, 29, 30, 45
    John, 130
Franey
    Benjamin, 96
Frankfurt Cottage, 82, 88, 89, 90
Franklin
    Joseph, 153
Franklyn
    Joseph, 110
Fry
    Thomas, 88, 89

Gaffney
    Charles, 170
Galloway
    Susannah and Frederick, 78
Gapp
    Edward, 149
    Frederick, 149
Garden Cottage, 19
Garwood
    William, 42, 43
Geary
    William, 171
George
    James, 156
Gibson

William, 39
Gillam
    Charles F, 20
Glass
    Annie, 110
Glebe Cottage, 126
Glenister
    John, 44
Glover
    Anne, 73, 200
Goddard
    Henry, 163
Godfrey
    Frederick, 119
Godfrey Way, 126
Goldsmith
    Harriet, 41
    Thomas, 41
Gosling's Cottages, 165
Gospel Hall
    The, 171
Gostling
    Augustus, 80
    Miss Maria, 43, 44, 63, 72, 80
Gostling House, 43
Gostling-Murray
    Colonel, 43, 165
Gotha House, 80, 82. See Woodside
    House. See Woodside House
Grafton Close, 130
Grasmere Avenue, 71
Green
    Emma, 31, 45, 56, 60, 87
    Thomas Haydon, 87
Greenbank
    Harry, 45, 180
    Lena, 45
    Walter, 180
Griffiths
    Charles, 163
    Eliza, 163
Grosmont, 21, 22
Grove
    The, 149
Groves
    John, 26

Grumett
    Edward, 97
Gunpowder Mills, 6, 92, 121, 131,
    135, 154, 156

Hackle
    Harry, 39
Hall Farm Drive, 174
Hamilton
    George, 113
    Thomas, 109
    William, 155
Hanworth Lodge, 130
Hanworth Park, 130
Hanworth Road, 6, 11, 117, 120,
    122, 124, 126, 128, 130, 138,
    141, 169
Harbon
    Joseph, 81
Harris
    Frederick, 110
    Harry, 43
Harwood
    Arthur, 83, 88
Hassan
    Sayad, 82
Hathway
    Sarah, 107
Hawkin
    Francis, 28, 30
Hawtayne
    Rev. W G, 79, 88
Head
    Thomas, 29, 78
Hearth Tax, 23, 185
Heath Cottage, 113
Heath Farm, 122
Heath Villa, 113
Heathfield Farm, 122
Heathfield Library, 140, 142
Heathfield Recreation Ground, 138
Heathfield School, 139
Hedges
    Emily, 152
Herbert

William, 175
Heston & Isleworth UDC, 74
Hewitt
    Richard, 155
    Sarah, 182
Higgins
    Joseph, 73
Higgs
    George, 31, 83
High Street
    Whitton, 146, 149
High Street, Hounslow, 7, 14, 15
Hill
    Mary, 60, 74
    Olive, 181
Hillier
    Thomas, 111
Hills
    George, 83
    Mary, 117
Holden
    Anne, 81
Holding
    Frank, 60
Holland
    Emily, 98
Holloway
    Sydney, 118
Holly Bush Corner, 6, 76, 97, 98,
    99, 102, 104, 163, 174, 179
Holt
    Charlotte & Lillian, 172
    James, 172
Hooper
    Frederick, 74
Hope
    Sarah, 84, 85, 150
Hope & Anchor Cottages, 150
Hope Cottages, 109
Horne
    John, 181
Hospital Bridge, 139
Hospital Bridge Road, 31, 117, 118,
    120, 139, 140, 142, 169, 177,
    187, 194, 195
Hospital Field, 140

Houghton
    Mildred, 80
Hounslow Cemetery, 125
Hounslow Heath, 122
Hounslow Loop
    The, 117
Hounslow Road, 6, 32, 49, 63, 65,
    67, 76, 78, 79, 82, 83, 84, 89,
    91, 93, 95, 102, 121, 171, 187,
    188, 193
Hughes
    Edward, 107
Hume Cottages, 150
Humphries
    Alfred, 118
Hunt
    Richard, 93, 94
Hyde
    John, 45
    Susannah, 45
Hyde's Cottage, 44, 45
Hyde's Cottages, 44, 45, 48
Hymen
    Eliza, 74

Ideal Homesteads Ltd, 132
Ilay
    Lord, 54
Imperial Café
    The, 91
Irving
    Sir Henry, 60, 61
Isolation Hospital, 119

James
    Mrs E, 167
James Walker, 19
Jessy Cottages, 82
Johnson
    Richard, 81
Jones
    Albert, 155
    Charles, 141
Jouvet

Emilie, 73
Jubilee Cottage, 179
Jubilee Farm, 146
Jury
  William, 168

Keith
  Sydney, 115
Kershaw
  Stanley, 78
Kerswell Community and Scout
  Hall, 70
Keswick Road, 67
Ketchell
  James, 152
  Stephen, 152
King
  George, 163
  Henry, 157
King's Cottage, 163
Kingsbury Cottage, 111
Kneller
  Sir Godfrey, 23, 88
Kneller Cottage, 32
Kneller Hall, 6, 17, 19, 24, 25, 28,
  30, 34, 36, 79, 88, 102, 104,
  110, 111, 118, 141, 144, 161,
  188, 192, 199, 200, 202
Kneller Road, 6, 11, 19, 20, 21, 24,
  31, 32, 34, 36, 37, 38, 39, 40,
  42, 44, 46, 49, 51, 52, 53, 55,
  59, 60, 78, 146, 165, 172, 174,
  176, 179, 187, 188, 193, 195
Kneller Villas, 49
Knight
  John, 131
Knighton
  Arthur, 87
Knights Hospitallers, 139
Knox
  Margaret, 78
Kyezor
  Louis, 62, 79, 80, 81, 82, 84, 87,
  88, 89, 90, 91, 95, 103, 110,
  167, 168, 169, 170, 194, 197,

201
  Matilda, 110
Kyezor Place, 80
Kyezor Terrace, 167
Kyezor Villas, 110
  Lancett
  George, 102
  John, 102

Langley
  George, 131
Lavesock
  Albert, 88
Leaver
  Benjamin, 149
Leggins
  Arthur, 155
Lewis
  Walter, 39, 96
Liddendale
  Frances, 96
Liddle
  Silas, 87
Lindsay
  James, 170
Locke
  Robert, 128
Loftie
  W J, 144
London City Mission, 171
Lynch Hill Terrace, 176

Mack
  Alfred, 49
Mahoney
  Frederick, 29
Mann
  Charlotte, 31, 175
  James, 175
  Walter, 175
Manns Cottages, 170
Manor House
  The, 36
Marble Hill Park, 74

Market Place
   The, 37, 181
Martin
   Frances, 30, 40
Matilda Cottages, 82, 87, 88, 90
Matthews
   Ben, 117
May Tree Cottage, 113
Maystrom
   James, 113
Meacock
   Edwin, 43
Meadway, 146
Meapham
   James, 152
Messenger
   Joseph, 60, 109
Metropolitan Public Gardens
   Association, 74
Mill Farm Business Park, 128
Minton
   James, 84
Mitchell
   James, 97, 102
Montrose Avenue, 146
Moss
   Frederick, 73
Murden
   Jeremiah, 47
Murphy
   Johanna, 156
   William, 111
Murray
   Charles Edward. *See* Colonel
   Murray
Murray Park, 37, 43, 49, 54, 55, 83,
   188
Murray's Cottage, 184
Murray's cottages, 91

Nash
   John, 183
Neal
   James, 113
Neale

Charles, 122
George, 183
Nelson Cottages, 106, 157
Nelson Gardens, 123
Nelson Road, 3, 6, 32, 37, 38, 78,
   102, 105, 106, 108, 110, 111,
   113, 114, 116, 117, 120, 122,
   123, 140, 161, 162, 163, 164,
   165, 166, 167, 169, 170, 171,
   174, 180, 181, 182, 184, 187,
   189, 195
Nelson School, 67
Nelson Villas, 165
Nevell
   Phillis, 160
   Thomas, 104
Nevell Cottages, 105
Nevells
   Alfred, 97, 98, 104
   George, 104
Nevells Place, 157
Neville
   Peter, 103
Neville Cottages, 157
Nevils Cottages, 96
Newson
   William, 78
Norris
   William Daniel, 26
Notts
   Charles, 26
Notts Cottages, 150
Nurseries
   The, 117

O'Neill
   Edmond, 110
Odd Manns Cottages, 157
Old Latmerians Sports Ground, 67
Old Riding School, 54
Old School, 32
Owen
   Richard, 110
   Sophia, 149
Oxford Cottage, 149

Parec Cottage, 184
Parfitt
  Eliza, 83
Park Avenue, 76
Park Place, 82, 83, 84, 87, 88, 89,
  90
Park Terrace, 110
Parker
  John, 102
Parris
  George, 184
Pauline Crescent, 149
Pavett
  Henry, 46
Payne
  Ernest, 155
  William, 94
Peacock
  Frank, 31, 32, 83, 146, 195
Pearce
  Charles, 154
  James, 91, 94, 106, 201
Pearce's Road, 91
Peck
  Elizabeth, 155
  Thomas, 26
Pemberton
  Daniel, 98, 119
Percy Road, 6, 31, 78, 122, 140,
  144, 145, 146, 147, 149, 150,
  151, 153, 154, 179, 195
Perkins
  Henry, 130
Philpot
  John, 189
Philpott
  George, 110
Phoenix Brewery, 26
Pigott
  Nathaniel, 24, 37
Pigsty Rookery, 80, 82
Pink, 118
  William, 118
Pocock
  Allan, 152
Pollington

James, 109
Pooley
  Jane, 94
Pope
  Alexander, 24, 37
Pope's Cottages, 182
Post Office, 39, 40, 41, 44, 126,
  134, 135, 172, 173, 201
Post Office Cottages, 44
Postman's Rest, 180
Poupart, 147
Powder Mill Cottages, 130
Powder Mill Lane, 130, 138
Powder Mill Lodge, 130
Prime
  Sir Samuel, 23, 24
Prince Albert public house, 81
Prospect Crescent, 52, 164, 166, 195
Prosser
  Rev. H P, 192
Pullen
  Edward, 147
  James, 86
  Wallace, 86

Rabbitt
  Charles S D, 142
Railway Cottage, 124
Railway Cottages, 118
Rainer
  Tom, 118
Randall
  Jesse, 89
Red Lion public house, 37
Red Lion public House, 181
Redway Estate, 142
Reeves
  George, 84, 158
Rose, 160
  William, 84
Repton
  Humphrey, 23
Retreat
  The, 112
Retreat Cottage, 180

Retreat Cottages, 173
Richie
    James, 113
Ridge
    The, 175
Ritz
    The, 62
River Colne, 11
River Crane, 11, 122, 139, 140
Roak
    Mary, 156
Robinson
    Rev. George C, 60
    Rev. R G, 119
    Stephen, 60
Rodgers
    Oliver, 89
Rodney Road, 118
Rogers
    James, 44
    Sarah, 183
Rosalind Villa, 122
Rose
    Arthur, 107
Rose Cottage, 110, 113
Roseam
    Ann, 105
Rosecroft Gardens, 19
Rosedale, 116
Ross Road, 147
Rossiter
    Mary, 117
Royal Military School of Music
    Kneller Hall, 20, 79, 102, 135, 202
Ruddock
    Joseph, 31
Rudduck
    Ann, 31
Rugby Football Union, 18, 31
Runnymede Road, 67
Rydal Gardens, 67

Sainsbury
    Emma, 97, 104

Salliesfield, 22
Salter
    Ellen May, 87
Scott
    George, 118
    Mansell, 163
Seale Hayne, M.P
    Hon. Charles, 11
Shaw-Hillier
    Thomas Bradney, 29
Shead
    Rebecca, 117
Shepherd, 84
Shot Tower, 132
Sich
    John & Henry, 46
Silwood
    James & Caroline, 54
Simms
    Edith, 154
Simpson Road, 124
Smail
    Eliza, 73
Smallhouse
    John, 46
Smith
    Henry, 152
    John, 188
Snell
    Peter, 156
Snowfield
    Florence, 74
South Lodge, 102
South Middlesex Isolation Hospital, 120
South Western Cottages, 118
Spanswick
    William, 130
Spiers
    Francis, 130
Spindler
    William, 42
Squelsh
    Sarah, 29
St Joseph's Villas, 166
St Philip and St James, 34, 60, 62,

63, 67, 79, 119, 141
St Philip and St James' School, 34
St. Augustine's Church, 140
St. Edmund of Canterbury, 112
St. John's Hospital, 59
Staines Road, 147
Stanhope Terrace, 95, 96
Statue
    The, 184
Steele
    Thomas, 88
Steptoe
    Richard, 154
Stevens
    George, 119
Stickley
    Ellen, 191
Strathearn Avenue, 147
Strokham
    John, 113
Suckling
    Dr Maurice, 103
    Sir John, 103
Swaker
    R W, 186
Swiss Cottage, 81, 82, 89, 90
Sydenham
    Dr, 59

Taplow Terrace, 176
Tewkesbury
    Philip, 111
Thomas Villas, 157
Thompson
    Fredreick, 170
Tithe Farm, 117
Townsend
    George, 117
Trafalgar House, 114
Tranmere Road, 157
Triangle Café, 37, 105, 181
Truce
    Sarah, 94
Twickenham Cemetery, 141
Twining

Elizabeth, 59
Richard, 59

Underwood
    John, 46

Vaughn
    H S, 144
Vicarage
    The, 6, 59, 60, 65, 67, 91
Vicarage Cottage, 59
Vicary
    Eliza, 94
Vicky Burke School of Dancing, 102
Vincam Close, 118
Volunteer Rifle Corps, 56

Walker
    James, 19
Walpole
    Horace, 62, 128
Ward
    Frederick, 153
Warner
    John, 83
Warren
    George, 188
    The, 175
Warren Farm, 147, 175
Warren Road, 24, 32, 174, 175,
    179, 195
Watson
    Emma, 109
Watts
    Thomas, 189
Webb
    Elizabeth, 73, 202
Wellington Road, 122
Wells Cottages, 118
West
    Elizabeth, 165
    Stephen, 165
Westeria Place, 107

Weston
    Harold, 45
Wheeler
    Elizabeth, 157
    John, 157
White
    William, 42, 43, 46, 87
White Hart Cottages, 42, 43, 187
White Hart Inn, 46
White Hart public House, 42
Whitear
    Sergeant, 29
Whitfield
    Louisa, 73
Whitton Clinic, 139
Whitton Dean, 5, 36, 37, 39, 40, 54, 55, 67, 83, 135, 179, 188, 189, 194
Whitton Dean Farm, 37, 177
Whitton Dene, 18, 36, 55, 76
Whitton Methodist Church, 148
Whitton Park Estate, 51, 54, 63, 80, 165, 188, 199
Whitton Park House, 71
Whitton Park railway station, 56
Whitton Park Sporting Club, 74
Whitton Park Terrace, 76, 77, 78, 188, 189
Whitton Railway Curve
    The, 117
Whitton Road, 11, 15, 18, 56, 76
Whitton School, 140
Whitton village, 31, 33, 36, 37, 161, 164, 179
Whitton Villas, 93, 94, 95
Williams
    David, 110
    Elizabeth Anne, 54, 202
Wills
    James, 43, 55, 69, 72, 74, 76, 165
Wills Crescent, 69
Wilson
    Alfred, 22
    Ann, 156
    Robert, 156

Wiltshire
    Mary, 31, 85
Windibank
    Richard, 92
Winning Post public house, 148
Woodbine Cottages, 150
Woodland
    Stephen, 26
Woodside House, 80, 81, 110
Woodside Villas, 110
Woodward
    Alfred, 176
    Arthur, 30, 37, 176, 177, 179
Woodward Cottage, 30, 37, 176
Woolgar
    John, 54
Woolroph
    Emily, 115
Wren
    Sir Christopher, 23
Wyndham Crescent, 122

Young
    Mabel, 164
    Malcolm, 44
    William, 168